PRAISE FOR *BEFORE THE BROOM*

"Psychologists Erica Holmes, Ronecia Lark, and Jessica M. Smedley have filled a much-needed void with this outstanding workbook for Black couples! The authors have simplified complex therapeutic concepts, making them accessible to couples by providing exercises that make generational connections. This is an indispensable resource for Black couples and therapists who work with Black couples."

—Yamonte Cooper, EdD, professor of counseling, El Camino College

"It is rare to find a resource that helps couples explore the intersection of spirituality, practicality, psychology, and ethnicity as a starting point for a meaningful, God-honoring marriage. Such is the case in this valuable ministry tool for pastors, counselors, and lovers. Here is helpful, instructional, and inspirational roadside information on the journey to the altar. Read it, share it, practice it before the vows, before the altar, *Before the Broom*."

—Kenneth C. Ulmer, DMin, PhD, senior advisor to the president at Biola University

"The collective wisdom of the psychologists who have penned this book is definitely at work! They understand the effects of historical trauma and use their knowledge to buttress our understanding of the nuances of Black culture in relation to Black love. They highlight the status of Black love and relationships, provide a blueprint to avoid the pitfalls that lead to heartache, and offer an honest view of the complexity of Black love. The authors also skillfully help us deal with and work to heal the crippling malady we collectively grapple with because of intergenerational racial trauma. In so doing, they carefully guide us toward a path paved with the sanctity of love. As the doctors masterfully step out of the intellectual space, they make concepts and interventions practical, affirming the beauty of Black love!"

—Kamilah Marie Woodson, PhD; author of *Colorism: Investigating a Global Phenomenon*; chair of the Department of Human Development and Psychoeducational Studies, School of Education, Howard University

"A most remarkable and timely tool for clinicians working with African American couples, for the couples themselves, and for African Americans desiring to be coupled! This culturally responsible achievement is a treasure. It not only investigates the relationship dynamics unique to African American couples, but it also discusses the sociohistorical factors that foster African American couples' development and the ways these factors currently impact the couples' relational patterns—down to the nuanced language. Doing transformative work with this population requires both a working knowledge of the cultural and contextual realities of African Americans and the skills to help couples explore, navigate, and negotiate these realities to curate healthy and sustainable intimate connections. This workbook charts the course for such necessary work. Bravo!"

—Jannis Moody, PhD; clinical psychologist; owner of Dr. Jannis Moody PLLC

"The authors have created a workbook for 'engaged' Black couples, designed to help them reflect on and discuss beliefs each partner holds. Completing the workbook together will help both partners understand the other on a deeper and more transparent level to determine whether their belief systems align as much as their intense physical attraction."

—William E. Cross Jr., professor emeritus in Counseling
Psychology, University of Denver

A PREMARITAL WORKBOOK
for DATING, ENGAGED, *and*
NEWLY MARRIED AFRICAN
AMERICAN COUPLES

DR. ERICA HOLMES, DR. RONECIA LARK,
and DR. JESSICA M. SMEDLEY

OVER NORTH
PUBLISHING

Information from "Patterns of African American Identity Development: A Life Span Perspective," by William E. Cross Jr. and Peony Fhagen-Smith, in *New Perspectives on Racial Identity Development: A Theoretical and Practical Anthology* has been used with permission by William E. Cross Jr.

Information about the communication types known as the Four Horseman of the Apocalypse and their antidotes has been used with permission by John Gottman and Julie Schwartz Gottman.

Published by Over North Publishing, Los Angeles

Edited and designed by Girl Friday Productions
www.girlfridayproductions.com

Book design: Rachel Marek
Project management: Sara Addicott and Laura Dailey
Image credits: © Wirestock/Shutterstock (cover image), © jasmine/ Adobe Stock (Sankofa), © SimeonVD/Shutterstock (rings)

ISBN (paperback): 978-1-7332320-2-9
ISBN (e-book): 978-1-7332320-3-6

Library of Congress Control Number: 2022922678

First edition

This book is dedicated to those who came before us, those who continue to walk beside us, and the generations that will come after us. Ashe.

CONTENTS

HOW TO USE THIS BOOK

*S*imply put, the aim of this workbook is to facilitate self-reflection and communication between you and your partner. By reflecting on your experiences, current practices, and future desires, you will be better able to convey those to your partner and discover areas of commonality, difference, and growth. Whether you are currently engaged or seriously dating, increased communication can lead to greater relational satisfaction now, greater marital satisfaction later, and overall feelings of connection. Our goal is to provide you with information to increase your knowledge of the correlation between experiences of *racial oppression* in the United States and our intimate relationships, increase personal insight, and enable you to make conscious relational choices. All three of us are licensed psychologists with expertise and training in couples therapy, and we have drawn on our extensive professional experience to guide you through content on avoiding and working through common relational and marital conflicts, to have a sustainable and satisfying marriage.

BEFORE YOU USE THIS BOOK

In preparation for beginning the workbook, there are a few things to consider.

Proceed with or without Assistance

You and your partner may choose to complete this workbook on your own or seek professional help to facilitate the processing of the exercises. This workbook can be approached as a strictly self-help text. You and your partner can work through the exercises as a couple and discuss the findings between yourselves. Alternatively, you and your partner can find a layperson (like a pastor) or licensed professional to assist you in a deeper exploration of your relationship. Either way, you both should decide on which format would work best for you as you begin.

Buy Two Copies

This workbook is intended to be completed by individuals who are in a serious dating relationship or who are currently engaged. Some of the exercises will focus on individual thoughts and experiences, and others will explore your current behaviors or future marital desires; therefore, each of you will need your own copy of the book to record your answers and complete the exercises.

Complete One Chapter per Week

This workbook is divided into eight distinct but related chapters. The idea is to complete one chapter weekly for eight weeks. Working through the book for eight consecutive weeks will help to facilitate an integration of the material as a whole and increase the likelihood that you and your partner will complete the entire book in a reasonable amount of time. Know that you do not have to complete the chapters in order. If you know that some chapters are more relevant to your current relationship than others, begin with those.

Schedule Time Daily

Given that this workbook is filled with numerous exercises for you to complete individually, we suggest that you schedule time to work on your current chapter daily. Time is a luxury for many. There never seem to be enough hours in the day to get through our to-do lists before we collapse for the evening. However, we ask you to make an eight-week commitment to prioritize your relationship. This might mean waking up an hour earlier before starting your daily routine, having a working lunch with your workbook, or picking up your workbook instead of the television remote. Before you begin, identify a time each day to devote to completing the exercises.

Schedule Weekly Time with Your Partner

We suggest scheduling time at the end of each week to review the exercises in your completed chapter together. This could be thought of as a reimagined date night for the next eight weeks. Calendaring a definite day and time each week to review your work together increases the likelihood that you will complete your chapters on your own and decreases the chance that other responsibilities will take priority. It further demonstrates your commitment, in that you both have set aside time to focus on each other and invest in your relationship.

OVERALL BOOK STRUCTURE

This workbook's eight chapters use the sociocultural contextual history of African Americans as a foundation on which to build a framework that thoroughly and systematically identifies essential focus areas. We researched literature on the impact of this history on relational functioning and selected each topic based on those findings.

The book is designed to provide information about the impact of institutionalized racism in each area and encourages self-reflection about how your experiences of racism have been individually internalized and shape relational dynamics. The book further encourages couples to identify and build on inherent strengths in their relationship.

The chapters, which cover distinct—yet connected—relational issues, are relatively brief and straightforward. The bulk of each chapter consists of exercises for you and your partner to complete alone and compare together.

Structure of Each Chapter

Each chapter is designed to be a self-contained lesson on a particular topic found to be important in premarital education. The chapters may therefore be read in any order. However, for simplicity, we do suggest that you go through the chapters in the order presented. If you find that there are more-pressing issues affecting your relationship currently, you can choose to begin with the chapters that are most relevant. Although each chapter topic was selected based on its demonstrated applicability to African American couples, given the research, you and your partner might find that some topics have more significance to your relationship than others. However, don't be surprised if, after completing a chapter and reviewing with your mate, you discover that the subject matter is of greater importance than you initially thought. For example, we are aware that chapter 6, "Blended (Dating with Children)," might not apply to everyone's relationship. If neither of you is bringing biological children into the relationship, you might spend time thinking about your relationship and connections to the children of your ex-partners or to the children of family members for whom you have responsibilities that might be integrated into your marriage.

The Concept of Sankofa

Each chapter is divided into three sections using the concept of *Sankofa*, a metaphorical symbol used by the Akan people of Ghana, West Africa. Sankofa is commonly depicted as either a bird with its head turned backward taking an egg from its back or an ornate stylized heart and translates as "go back and get it." It expresses the significance of reaching back to knowledge gained in the past and bringing it into the present to make positive progress. Sankofa emphasizes the equal importance of three points in time: past, present, and future. This worldview aligns with the way we work with couples in our respective practices. We use this same framework to structure each chapter. You begin with exercises aimed at reflecting on the past. You then transition to exercises focused on current practices and beliefs. The final section allows you to consider your desires and expectations for your future marriage.

Glossary of Terms

Last, a glossary is included as appendix C to help define terms that you might not be familiar with. As you read, you will notice that the terms included in the glossary are *italicized* for easy recognition when first mentioned. The words are listed in alphabetical order in the glossary, not in the order they appear in the text.

A NOTE ABOUT LANGUAGE

To begin, we would like to address the use of the term "African American" in the subtitle and throughout the workbook. This term was deliberately chosen to underscore the fact that this book was written with consideration of the historical context and experiences of American-born Black people whose ancestry dates back to *enslavement*. This was not done to exclude our brothers and sisters across the *diaspora* and around the globe but is an attempt to recognize and honor the unique within-group experiences we have. The history, statistics, and marriage perspectives that are shared in each chapter are based in a US context and may or may not speak to the experiences of those in other countries. We hope that Black people, regardless of location, will find this information to be helpful. You will also notice that throughout the book we use "African American" and "Black" interchangeably. We understand the power of language and seek to connect us rather than divide us.

Last, yes, we capitalize the word "Black" but not "white" when referring to racial, ethnic, or cultural terms. Debates about whether to capitalize both or neither are ongoing in the journalism world. We agree with many who state that capitalizing the term "white" as done by white supremacists risks covertly reinforcing those beliefs. Capitalizing "Black" underscores a shared sense of history, identity, and community among people who identify as Black across the globe.

THE ALLEGORY OF THE HAM

Author Unknown

A woman was in the kitchen cooking a birthday dinner for her husband and a few invited guests. One of the guests came into the kitchen to offer a hand and noticed something a bit strange. She asked the cook, "What happened to this end of the ham?" The cook replied, "Oh, I cut it off before I cooked it." The guest asked the cook why she would cut off the end of the ham before putting it in the oven. She thought of many possibilities: Does it help the ham cook faster or more evenly? Does it help the juices mix with the brown sugar? To her surprise, the cook said, "I have no idea. This is the way my mom always cooked ham when I was growing up, and it came out delicious every time." They both shrugged, finished up in the kitchen, and continued with the party. However, after the party ended and things settled down, the cook became curious about ham cooking. The next morning it was still on her mind, so she called her mom and asked, "Mom, why do we cut off the end of the ham before we cook it?" The mother answered, "Well, honey, I don't know. That's how my mom, your granny, taught me to cook a ham." The mom offered to call her mother to get the answer and solve the mystery. The mom called granny and asked, "Mom, why do we cut off the end of the ham before we cook it? Your granddaughter called and asked me, and I told her that I learned that from you." Granny responded, "Well, I don't know why y'all cut the end off of your ham, but I did that because I didn't have a pan large enough to fit a whole ham back then."

The *allegory* of the ham illustrates how ways of being and doing are passed down in families. Often undiscussed and unquestioned, they become "normal" or "the right way" and are used to judge others: "This ham doesn't taste good because the end wasn't cut off."

We have to be careful because what was once done for survival can become ingrained—a blueprint for the way we move throughout our lives and relationships. This is intensified when an entire culture had to learn to survive near annihilation. However, those same techniques that helped our ancestors survive may not be helpful in our present-day circumstances. Maybe there is no need to cut off the end of the ham anymore.

INTRODUCTION

*P*resent-day discussions about marriage in the African American community are colored by a myriad of thoughts, beliefs, and reactions. Commentary is often littered with skepticism and doubt, optimism and anticipation, apprehension and fear, fantasy and naivete. When questioned, most singles admit that they never received any structured education about relationships or marriage: they learned what they currently know from observing their parents' relationships while growing up and from their own relational experiences as adults. Sadly, this does not bode well for most.

Over the past few decades, there have been shifts in both marriage rates and marriage trends, especially for African Americans. Upon reflection, many reading this workbook may realize major differences in ideas about marriage between their parents' generation and their own. Marriage rates for African Americans have historically been lower than for other ethnic groups and have continually declined over the years. Today, less than half of African Americans are married. The gap in marriage rates between Blacks and other ethnic groups has not always been as prevalent as this. During enslavement, the Black enslaved engaged in plantation marriages that, although not legally recognized, were considered bonded unions. Once marriage was legalized post-enslavement, marriage rates among African American men and women were extremely high. However, by the late 1980s, the marriage rate for African Americans dropped drastically. Currently, African Americans have lower marriage rates than any other ethnic group in the United States, indicating that they are the least likely to get married. Despite the decrease in African American marriages, research has shown that African Americans continue to place a high value on marriage and continue to desire marriage.

So, what accounts for this difference? Communal experiences such as *historical* and *cultural oppression* have had an impact on marriage and divorce rates among African Americans, attitudes about marriage, when to get married, and even whether to get married. Further, Black women who choose to marry do so much later in life and are more likely to divorce than any other ethnic group. To increase the chances to marry and have a successful marriage, a contextual understanding of the threats to African American marriages is necessary. The fact that experiences of racism, *discrimination*, and *oppression* have profoundly shaped and significantly affected the African American couple must be acknowledged, along with learning new and healthier ways to address the legacy of pain and *trauma* that invades interactions.

Some people may stop reading right now because "slavery was so long ago, why do we have to keep bringing it up"; "what happened during slavery is just an excuse for the bad behavior of 'Negroes' today"; "what happened during slavery has nothing to do with me because I'm educated, successful, and have overcome"; or you fill in the blank. However, the trauma of enslavement still lives in each of us descendants. Neither we nor our ancestors have ever been given an opportunity to grieve or process what we experienced, and the effects of that have been felt for generations. The research on *intergenerational trauma* is clear: trauma that is not processed is present, and trauma that is present is passed down. This is especially true for descendants of American enslavement for whom the atrocities were never addressed and for whom racial injustices persist. Many scholars have discussed how the legacy of American enslavement and oppression have affected both African American men and women and subsequently their relationships when coupled. However, this information is not widely available or known to those in the general public. Therefore, many are left uninformed and ill-equipped to handle marital conflicts that might arise.

Some may ask, Why is it important to encourage African Americans to marry? There are numerous reasons for African Americans to marry: For example, research has found that those who marry live longer, on average, and tend to be physically healthier than those who never marry or those who divorce. Marriage has also been demonstrated to have a positive impact on wealth attainment, mental health, and social status. This workbook is not intended to persuade people to get married. Rather, we would like to increase the likelihood for a healthy and satisfying marriage for those who desire marriage.

WORKBOOK GOALS

The goals of this workbook can be summed up by one word: SAVE.

This workbook will help you SAVE by:

- *S*—Strengthening your communication and relational connection through increased awareness, self-reflection, and vulnerability.
- *A*—Assessing the compatibility of your values, desires, ability to work

through differences, and willingness to compromise.

- *V*—Validating your decision to date, to commit to the relationship, to take a break, or to leave the relationship all together. At the completion of this workbook:
  - some will decide not to get married = success;
  - some will decide to wait to get married = success;
  - some will decide to set a date = success.
- *E*—Enjoying getting to know each other and yourself.

As a result of completing this book with your partner, we hope that you SAVE time, energy, frustration, and heartbreak.

Save time by focusing on the areas of a relationship known to be associated with high conflict and correlated with relationship satisfaction. Completing the questions in each chapter can assist you in making decisions about the viability of your relationship in eight weeks, rather than in eight months.

Save energy by engaging in focused activities that can help you identify underlying issues that might be disguised as other things but that cause conflict in your relationship.

Save frustration by gaining an understanding of how your family histories have influenced the ways you and your partner show up in the relationship and by learning healthy ways to communicate about areas of difference and conflict.

Save heartbreak by engaging both your thinking brain and your emotional brain in making decisions about the future of your relationship. By making conscious decisions about what you need, what you want, and how to get it, you can be intentional about how and if your relationship proceeds.

Before you begin this workbook, sit down with your partner and decide what day and time you two will set aside each week to review each chapter. To keep it simple, try to schedule the same day and time each week, if possible.

Record your plan below:

We will meet (in person—by phone/FaceTime—by video)
(circle one)

on _____ at _____ a.m./p.m. each week.
(day of the week)   *(time)*

Complete your planning by discussing and answering the following questions. These will help to ensure clarity and reduce the need to come up with alternatives in the moment.

1. If you are meeting in person, where will you meet?
   - Will you meet at each other's homes? If you don't live together, will you alternate?
   - Will you meet in another location? Your favorite coffee spot, a park, the beach, a restaurant?
2. If you meet by phone/FaceTime, who will initiate the call? Will you alternate weekly?
3. If you meet by video conference, who will set up and share the video link? Will you use the same link for all eight discussions?
4. How will the need to reschedule be communicated?
   - If there is a need to reschedule, you should pick a new day and time within forty-eight hours.
5. List other details to clarify before you get started below.

_____
_____
_____
_____
_____
_____
_____
_____
_____
_____
_____
_____
_____
_____
_____
_____
_____

 Note: Some exercises are marked with a special symbol that looks like two wedding rings. These exercises are extremely important to answer and discuss with your partner. If you find that you don't have enough time to talk about all the exercises in a given chapter, prioritize these.

Before you get started, take some time to evaluate the strengths and growth areas in your relationship. Put a check mark under "Strength" or "Growth Area" for each item.

	Strength	Growth Area
We share thoughts and feelings and understand what the other is saying and means (*communication*).		
We are comfortable discussing our needs and desires for affection and sex (*intimacy* and *sex*).		
We agree on financial matters, including bills, credit, savings, and spending (*finances*).		
We are able to discuss and resolve differences (*conflict*).		
We hold similar religious values, beliefs, and practices (*spirituality*).		
We hold similar beliefs about what it means to be Black in America (*race* and *culture*).		
We balance activities together and apart well (hobbies and hangouts).		
Our relationships with each other's relatives and friends are good (*family* and *friends*).		
We agree on how to share decision-making and responsibilities (*roles* and *responsibilities*).		
Other:		
Other:		
Other:		

Resources for further information on Black marriages and marriage rates:

— Articles from the United States Census Bureau, such as this one: Gurrentz, Benjamin. "Cohabiting Partners Older, More Racially Diverse, More Educated, Higher Earners." United States Census Bureau, September 23, 2019. https://www.census.gov/library/stories/2019/09/unmarried-partners-more-diverse-than-20-years-ago.html.

— The National Center on African American Marriages and Parenting: https://www.hamptonu.edu/ncaamp/

— Black Demographics—The African American Population: https://blackdemographics.com/households/marriage-in-black-america/

CHAPTER 1

Who Am I? (Racial Identity)

e assume that one of the primary reasons you and your partner selected this premarital workbook rather than any other is because it was designed specifically for African Americans. Therefore, we also assume that both of you find significance and meaning in that aspect of your *personal identity* and at some level acknowledge that the African American experience is unique. Personal identity refers to your self-image and your beliefs about the kind of person you are and how you differ from others. This includes how you think about yourself, how you think about yourself in relation to others, and how you experience being perceived by the world around you. Simply put, we define personal identity by asking: Who am I? Who am I in relation to others? How does what others think about me have an impact on me? However, race is defined by the common physical characteristics of people of shared ancestry. For example, people with dark skin, tightly coiled hair, and a broader nose and lips are generally classified as "Black"—of African ancestry. Although there is no biological or scientific basis for "race," societies have created racial categories and have used them to divide humanity and create irrational hierarchies between groups of people. Think about personal identity as your internal thoughts about who you are and race as an external classification of what group you belong to. In this chapter, *racial identity* refers to the meaning, weight, and importance that being "African American/Black" has in your life. The degree of significance that your racial identity has will have an impact on how you approach, perceive, and respond to every aspect of your life, including your relationship.

Living while Black means that you likely have a unique set of historical, generational, and present-day experiences connected to race that you bring with you into your relationship. It is important to understand how your specific racial identity affects your decision-making, how you make meaning of your experiences, and your future plans.

To explore racial identity, we look to psychologist *William E. Cross Jr.,* who, since the 1960s, has dedicated his work to the study of racial identity development for the Black community. His work tells us that racial identity develops in sectors based on "racialized" experiences in the world. Our experiences with our family, our friends/peers, our community, and the larger society all help shape and give meaning to what it means to be "Black."

In 1971, Dr. Cross developed a theory for understanding Black racial identity called *nigrescence.* Nigrescence theory describes a process of becoming Black or developing a Black racial identity. In 2001, Dr. Cross collaborated with *Dr. Peony Fhagen-Smith* to revise his earlier theory to include how we are racially socialized over our life span. They highlight factors that contribute to varying levels of importance one places on their "Blackness." They further highlight how the importance one places on their race affects how they see and behave in the world.

We have summarized their ideas below. Read each sector and the accompanying examples carefully. There is a lot of information here (new information for some), so you might have to read it a few times.

MODEL OF BLACK IDENTITY DEVELOPMENT

The following discussion is based on "Patterns of African American Identity Development: A Life Span Perspective" by William E. Cross Jr. and Peony Fhagen-Smith.

Sector One: Infancy and Childhood in Early Black Identity Development

Early exposure of Black children occurs through contact with families, schools, churches, and historical events. Parents, caregivers, and those who are present in a child's life have routines and norms that represent Black culture. Young children are consistently being schooled in Black culture through observation and exposure. The Black child is unaware of racism at this time.

Sector Two: Preadolescence

Development in this sector is highly influenced by the parents' upbringing and the importance they put on being Black. During this time, identity types show up in three categories:

1. *High race importance* develops because parents openly instill the importance of being Black into the child. Black culture is most important, and what it means to be Black is openly discussed. For example, the parents openly talk about Black history, culture, and issues affecting Black people and the Black community. Being Black has meaning, and the family actively and openly acknowledges it.
2. *Low race importance* develops because the parents place no value on race or on being Black. The child is only aware of physical features. For example, the parents might talk about skin color or hair texture but do not talk about Black culture. The extreme might be "we are all part of the human race and that's all that matters."
3. *Internalized racism* occurs when being Black is looked at negatively among close family and there is a lack of desire to identify as Black. This results in negative views of the Black community, a belief in *stereotypes*, and thus the development of self-hatred. For example, parents might say negative things like "I want to move out of this neighborhood because Black people don't care about anything." We will discuss internalized racism in more detail at the end of this section.

Sector Three: Adolescence

During adolescence, a Black self-concept begins to develop. Peer/friend groups are very important, and the adolescent begins a process of self-exploration of Black identity. Individuals may confirm or redefine their race importance in this sector. Development during this time may be affected by a person's peer group, community, and school environment. For example, others may have a specific idea of what it means to be Black and how Black people should behave. They may use their beliefs to judge your Blackness or to call it into question. Should your "Black card" be revoked because you are not Black enough, or should we be embarrassed because you are too Black? Not being Black enough or being too Black can refer to the way you behave, your mannerisms, the way you speak, and your appearance.

Sector Four: Adult Nigrescence

Four stages accompany nigrescence (the process of becoming Black).

Stage	Description	Example
Pre-encounter	Individuals with low race importance* will try to blend into mainstream/white culture but may have a surface-level appreciation of Black culture. Individuals with internalized racism will become anti-Black. They see their Blackness as a negative aspect of themselves and will see white culture as "better" and as the standard.	The Black person is involved in all white spaces and activities and mostly with white people and may intentionally avoid experiences where there might be too many Black people. They may see white as "right" and Black as bad and inferior. They may say things like "Black people are ghetto and violent."
Encounter	The person in the *encounter* stage will experience an event or situation that will cause internal conflict and a questioning of their Black identity. This is characterized by an emotional personal experience, which fosters a need to change.	The Black person is out with a group of white friends, and they are stopped by the police. The police only ask the Black person for identification and question him about being there, while his white friends look on.
Immersion-Emersion (a two-step process)	As a result of the encounter stage, which fosters an awakening of sorts ("I'll never be white"), the person becomes *immersed* in Black culture. They may become pro-Black and entrench themselves in the culture and issues of the group. They may accept symbols illustrating Blackness (e.g., hair, clothes, music) and have a strong desire to reject "white culture" and white people. In the second phase, the person *emerges* from the intense emotionality of the first phase to develop a more balanced view of the Black community and becomes open to seeing the various sides of the community.	The person cuts their hair, begins to wear African clothing, only engages in "Black" social events and activities, and may move to an area with a relatively large concentration of Black residents. Then, the person slowly becomes more open to racially diverse groups and events and may begin to socialize with non-Black co-workers.

Stage	Description	Example
Internalization/ Internalization Commitment	After the transitional period of *emersion* is resolved, the person *internalizes* their new identity in a natural way. The person becomes secure within themselves and their Blackness. Last, the person is committed to putting their newly *internalized*, secure Black identity to work and begins to advocate for change.	The Black person begins to speak out when they see *anti-Black racism* happen—for example, telling a "Karen" to chill.

*Cross and Fhagen-Smith use the term *race salience*. We replaced the word "salience" with "importance" for simplicity.

 Thinking about adult nigrescence, what stage(s) are you in?

_____

 Your partner?

_____

The shadow of enslavement continues to rear itself in many different forms of racism. One of the symptoms of racism is our history of internalizing our oppression, often as a means of survival. The weight of internalized racism and oppression can cause us to have unrealistic expectations of ourselves and our partners. You might be wondering what we mean by "internalized racism." It means that as a community, many of us have historically believed and continue to believe the negative messages that we hear about our race (i.e., the stereotypes). Sadly, many of us act out those messages in our daily lives. For example, sometimes we have negative beliefs about skin color or hair texture, and those beliefs influence who we think is cute, date, or consider for marriage. Additionally, internalized racism will have an impact on the standards we set for ourselves ("This is all I deserve."), our belief systems ("Black men are cheaters." "Black women are mean."), and our physical appearance ("I'm too dark skinned." "I'm light skinned, so my hair should be straight and wavy."), and all these beliefs can show up in relationships.

Research has shown that the impact of internalized messages about race and colorism begins at very early stages of childhood development. Skin color has also been linked to self-esteem at early ages. The messages we hear about our color, especially for women, sometimes affect our expectations of our partners and how we show up in dating and marital relationships. Do we tend to base our attraction on skin color? Hair texture? Body shape or size? Do we try to strategically find a partner who will help us to produce "pretty babies" with "good hair"? Do we measure a certain level of

"Blackness" that we think is socially acceptable and criticize those who don't meet that arbitrary standard? These are just a few examples of how internalized messages about race and color affect our dating expectations.

Write down a few ways that internalized racism has affected how you feel about yourself and others. _____

_____

_____

_____

_____

_____

_____

THE PAST

As mentioned in the Model of Black Identity Development, early messages received about racial identity come from our surroundings. The *Clark Doll Study* highlighted the fact that negative messages about what it means to be Black begin at a very early age. Black children as young as kindergarten age often begin to act on negative messages and stereotypes about their race and skin color. These messages can be direct statements from our families: "Stay out of the sun or you're going to get Black." "She has good hair." They can also be indirect messages from the media when only Black people with "white" features are leads or Black people are shown in stereotypical roles (e.g., criminals or drug addicts). A lack of representation speaks just as loudly as selective representation. Thus, we begin to think about ourselves in racialized ways. We form beliefs about our looks, our abilities, what is expected of us, and where we belong. Representation is very important to developing racial identity, as it can foster a sense of belonging, offer positive role models, and help to counter damaging stereotypes. Sometimes representation can look like parents buying their children books with positive representations of Black people. It can occur through the experience of having a Black teacher or doctor in the community. Or on a larger scale, it can be the celebration of the first Black president and Black woman vice president in the United States.

As stated in the Cross and Fhagen-Smith model referenced above, during adolescence our friends begin to influence how we relate to our Blackness. At the same time, we explore who we are as individuals and how we define our identity relative to others in social and intimate relationships. Questions arise such as what it means to be "Black enough" or what it means to be worthy of a "Black card"; being questioned by our peers or experiencing isolation when we are in a situation where we are "the only one" shape our connection to our race.

As we move into early adulthood, similar themes continue and are affected by the environments in which we find ourselves, whether work settings, higher education, or geographic region. The way we maneuver through the world as a Black person will be revealed in our choices: who we befriend, where we live, and who we see as dateable.

As we know, not all experiences of racial identity development are positive. In many instances, Black people can identify an event, a message they heard from a parent or teacher, or some pivotal moment of discovering their race. This can result in negative associations of race, ultimately leading to racial trauma. We often think of trauma when we hear of war, abuse, or violence; but it is important to know that trauma is any sort of disruption of our sense of safety, especially within our own bodies and identities. Perhaps you were exposed to images that depicted Black people in a negative manner. Perhaps you heard messages uttered by your parents or elders that were soaked in internalized racism.

Take a moment to reflect on the following prompts that will explore your experiences of sector two (preadolescence) and sector three (adolescence) of the Model of Black Identity Development described in the previous section. Think about what events may have contributed to your journey of racial identity development.

 Think about your primary caregivers and the importance they put on race. Think about whether they openly talked about being Black and what it meant and how they talked about it. Rate their level of race importance by placing a check mark in the appropriate category. You can use the blank spaces to add additional relatives not listed (stepparents, play aunts and uncles, etc.).

Adults	High Race Importance	Low Race Importance	Internalized Racism
Grandmother			
Grandfather			
Grandmother			
Grandfather			
Mother			
Father			
Aunt			
Uncle			

What were some early messages you heard about your being Black from the adults in your family (parents, aunts, uncles, grandparents, other caregivers)?

_____

_____

_____

_____

_____

_____

List a few negative and positive examples of representation that you had when you were little (Black dolls, Black books, watching the local news).

_____

_____

_____

_____

_____

_____

Were there any stereotypes you heard early on about Black women and Black men that you now realize are rooted in internalized racism? _____

_____

_____

_____

_____

_____

Was your Blackness ever questioned or challenged? (For example, were you ever told that you weren't Black enough because of how you looked, talked, or where you grew up?) _____

_____

_____

_____

_____

_____

_____

THE PRESENT

Taking the time to explore the past can be a meaningful way to unveil our current decisions and patterns. Hopefully, you were able to make some meaningful connections by becoming familiar with the Model of Black Identity Development and reflecting on your past experiences. We will continue to explore how early racial identity development progresses over time and appears in adulthood and in your current relationship. If we reference the model and explore the adult transition stages (nigrescence) from early into full adulthood, we will notice that there are various shifts in how we identify the importance of race to our identity. For example, if you are in the pre-encounter stage and your partner is in the immersion-emersion stage, how you perceive racially involved events, cope with them, and talk about race will vary (refer back to "Sector Four: Adult Nigrescence" if necessary). You may also have different internalized beliefs that you are not aware of that will manifest in your approaches to communication, *intimacy*, and decision-making. The messages we heard early on about race shape how we think about race today and our beliefs about our communities and ourselves.

 Let's explore some of those messages by doing a bit of myth busting. Part of unpacking internalized racism is calling out toxic messages that we hold as normal and as the truth. Where do you currently fall? Place a check mark.

Myths to Unlearn . . .	Believe	Struggle Not to Believe	Disbelieve
"Nappy" hair is bad hair.			
It's pretty to be dark skinned.			
Black women aren't soft and loving.			
Black men/women are angry and aggressive.			
Black men are lazy.			
Baby mamas are money hungry.			
Baby daddies are deadbeats.			
Lighter skin = pretty baby.			
Black men don't have good credit.			
Black women are hard on Black men.			
Black women can cook.			
Black men are cheaters.			

Myths to Unlearn . . .	Believe	Struggle Not to Believe	Disbelieve
Black people don't engage in the fine arts.			
Black people don't travel.			
Black is beautiful.			
Racism is a thing of the past.			
Black men have big sex organs.			
Black people are targeted because we are great.			
Black people are poor.			

Now think about your partner. How do any of these myths resonate with whom you decide to date? Which of them drive your decision-making or expectations with your current partner? _____

_____

_____

_____

_____

_____

_____

_____

_____

_____

_____

_____

_____

_____

_____

_____

_____

_____

_____

_____

_____

_____

_____

_____

_____

_____

_____

_____

_____

_____

_____

_____

_____

_____

_____

Use the table below to note some of your preferences related to Black culture. Do you have real feelings about these?

	Okay	Maybe	Not Okay
Use the N-word?			
For women to wear natural hair?			
For women to wear processed hair, a weave, or a wig?			
Engage in protests (e.g., Black Lives Matter)?			
Take vaccines?			
Seek Western medicine?			
Celebrate Black cultural holidays (e.g., Juneteenth, Kwanzaa)?			
Celebrate Black cultural "heroes"?			
Being called Black?			
Being called African American?			

THE FUTURE

You have now explored the past and hopefully have a sense of the impact of old messages on your feelings about Blackness and how they may be harmful in your relationship. Now let's identify some goals for the future. It is imperative to have protective factors that celebrate your entire self, especially your race and ethnicity. It is time to consider how you want to continue on your journey of racial identity development, while implementing protective factors of resilience and strength. Perhaps there are some family memories that feel loving and healing. Perhaps there is an example or two of a relationship that you looked up to, but you haven't quite figured out how to intentionally integrate those parts into your relationship. Or maybe you have an idea about what types of messages you want to pass on to the next generation, should you decide to have children.

Here is a list of examples that you will explore for yourself and then talk to your partner about to see where you align and where you differ. Check the box with the response that best fits your opinion and desires for the given examples.

	Agree	Neutral	Disagree
Celebrating my Black heritage is important to me.			
Talking to our children about race is/will be important.			
Engaging in Black community organizations is important to me.			
I observe/celebrate MLK Day, Juneteenth, or Kwanzaa.			
My race is an important part of me.			
Engaging in a diverse, multicultural community is important (e.g., having friends of different races).			
I want to raise our children around other Black children.			
Representations of Black culture in the home are important to me.			
I would prefer for my children to attend predominantly Black schools.			

Racial identity is an imperative part of who you are and how you show up in your relationship. Continue to keep these things in mind as you complete each of the remaining chapters. Our race and our history have an impact on our experiences in the world, and this chapter lays the foundation for the other aspects of this work. How we understand ourselves as racial beings has a direct impact on our image of self, how we view ourselves in relation to others, our self-esteem, and how we view ourselves in the context of the larger society. It also shapes our expectations in relationships, as it dictates our thoughts and beliefs about what we have to offer and what we expect to receive. Identifying as African American or Black greatly shapes how we experience other domains of our lives. Whether with regard to our faith, finances, children, or intimacy, our racial identity bleeds into all aspects of our relationship journey.

As a result of your weekly discussion:

⊙⊙ Our identified strengths in this area are: _____

_____

_____

_____

_____

_____

⊙⊙ The things that we need to continue to talk about in this area are: _____

_____

_____

_____

_____

_____

⊙⊙ What are your next steps? How will you work on your growth areas? Write down your plan of action. For example, will you seek help from others (i.e., a counselor, therapist, or mentor), or will you two read, study, and discuss together as a couple? _____

_____

_____

_____

_____

_____

Resources for further information on racial identity:

- "Patterns of African American Identity Development: A Life Span Perspective" by William E. Cross Jr. and Peony Fhagen-Smith, in *New Perspectives on Racial Identity Development: A Theoretical and Practical Anthology,* edited by Charmaine L. Wijeyesinghe and Bailey W. Jackson III (New York University Press, 2001), pp. 243–70.
- *Shades of Black: Diversity in African-American Identity* by William E. Cross (1991).
- *Post Traumatic Slave Syndrome: America's Legacy of Enduring Injury and Healing* by Joy DeGruy (2017).
- *Why Are All the Black Kids Sitting Together in the Cafeteria? And Other Conversations About Race* by Beverly Daniel Tatum (2017).

CHAPTER 2

Higher Power
(Religion and Spirituality)

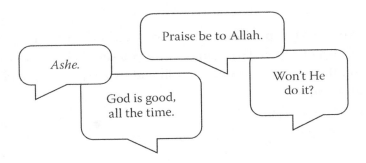

The African American community has a long history of connection and belief in a higher power. Be it God, Allah, a draw to the teaching of Buddha, or traditional West African religion, we have always had a sense of the divine and a relationship to something greater. Religious/spiritual beliefs shape the way that the "believer" interacts with and understands the world around them and their experiences. They shape ideas of right and wrong, an understanding of suffering and joy, and answers about the purpose of human existence and the meaning of life itself. In a way, religious/spiritual beliefs provide a code of conduct for how life "should be lived."

Although the United States is generally considered to be a highly religious nation, African Americans stand out as the most religiously committed racial group in the country, based on level of affiliation with a religion, attendance at religious services, frequency of prayer, and religion's importance in life. According to the Pew Research Center, nearly 90 percent of African Americans identify as religious, to some degree, and are absolute about the existence of a higher power. This is not surprising given that spirituality for Black folks goes back to our African roots, where we were/are highly invested in a connection to the greater universe, a higher power, and the land. It is the acknowledgment of and link to something greater than ourselves that contributes to our resilience.

Enslavement had an impact on the way the enslaved were able to practice their beliefs. Prior to enslavement, most Africans practiced traditional African religions; however, white enslavers began to convert them to Christianity once they were captured. This was done by force (beatings), through manipulation (only being allowed to gather "unsupervised" during Christian church service), and by controlling access to information (allowing the enslaved to learn to read by using the Bible). A 2020 survey by PRRI found that 72 percent of Black Americans still identified as Christian, belonging to varying denominations, with the majority of the descendants of American enslavement being Baptist. It is important to point out that identifying as Christian does not mean actively participating in Christianity. It does mean, however, that Christian principles influence the way they approach the world, to some degree. Whether you identify as Christian or not, you probably have an idea of what we mean when we say "the *Black church*." Regardless of how you feel about it (and its connection to enslavement), you must admit that the church has been instrumental in shaping us and our community. It has been a source of social, financial, educational, and political support to the community and, in many instances, continues to be. In the same vein, we must also acknowledge that we are not all the same nor do we all have the same experiences.

The experiences of Black people and their spirituality can exist in many forms—churches, mosques, synagogues, spiritual communities, traditional cultural practices, and many others—or may include no spiritual practices at all. For some, connection to a higher power has not been an important aspect of who they are. No matter the viewpoint, spiritual beliefs or the lack thereof influence attitudes and expectations about dating and marriage for both you and your partner. Couples who highly agree on spiritual beliefs report much higher levels of marital satisfaction and closeness than those with low spiritual agreement. Holding differing religious and spiritual beliefs may affect various areas of your life, such as views on domestic violence, *gender roles*, how conflict is managed, and ideas about divorce. Therefore, it is important for the two of you to discover and assess how compatible your spiritual beliefs are. Areas such as devoutness (how strictly you adhere to your religious heritage), interfaith (you belong to different faith groups, such as Catholic or Pentecostal), and significance (the importance you place on religion/spirituality) are important to explore. If you and your partner find areas where your spiritual beliefs are in conflict or are not compatible, talking about the origins and the importance of your beliefs can help you understand one another.

THE PAST

Our views about the world, our moral compass, and our rules for how we view relationships are often rooted in our religious or spiritual experiences during childhood. Family narratives and traditions from our parents/caregivers are sometimes good indicators of what belief system we were exposed to during childhood. Many of the messages we heard from our elders were passed down through generations and rooted in spiritual belief systems. Conversations held around dating, marriage, sex, and children were most likely grounded in an underlying religious/spiritual belief system. The goal of this section is to explore your past experiences with religion, spirituality, and faith and understand how those experiences shaped your early ideas of the world around you.

Describe the religious/spiritual practices of your family. What messages were given about religion/spirituality? _____

_____

_____

_____

_____

Describe a typical day of religious observance in your family's household (e.g., a typical Friday if your family practiced Judaism, a typical Saturday if you were raised Seventh-Day Adventist, a typical Sunday if you were raised Christian/Catholic, a typical day if you were raised as an *atheist*). _____

_____

_____

_____

_____

Sometimes we have unfortunate or painful experiences that come along with church or religion. Describe any "church hurt" or religious/spiritual community wounds you experienced in childhood. _____

_____

_____

_____

_____

THE PRESENT

Having a sense of your past influences can help you explore and be more aware of your present decisions and traditions as they relate to spiritual practices. It is also important to know and remain true to the things that are important to you. As mentioned previously, historically, spirituality and faith were grounding and have served as protective factors in our cultural experiences and resilience. However, we also know that things have changed in the twenty-first century. Many of us do not engage in the faith practices of our grandparents, or we do not practice in the way they did. We may have more- or less-rigid beliefs, views, interpretations, and practices than previous generations. Many of us have found more "modern" ways to experience our spiritual selves. Perhaps you engaged in a form of meditation or prayer as you were seeking your partner. Perhaps there are meaningful quotes or experiences in nature that you engage with in order to feel connected, or maybe you have upheld the religious practices of your family and desire to continue in that tradition. Whether you fall into any of these categories or not, including your partner in that part of you can create deeper intimacy and contribute to a deeper bond between you two.

How would you currently describe yourself spiritually/religiously? _____

_____

_____

_____

_____

How is that similar/different from how you were raised? _____

_____

_____

_____

_____

Are there things about your spiritual/religious/faith upbringing that you no longer support or find helpful to continue? If so, describe them. _____

_____

_____

_____

_____

_____

_____

❦ Is your partner a part of your current faith community/spiritual practices? If you have different belief systems, what do you need to discuss that you perhaps have been hesitant to address? _____

_____

_____

_____

_____

_____

_____

_____

_____

_____

❦ Now let's explore how your values and behaviors are shaped by your spiritual or religious beliefs or background. The more aware you are of these practices or beliefs, the better you can communicate them to your partner. For each topic or word provided, take a moment to write down some general rules that you have been taught and continue to follow.

Diet (include food you can and cannot eat, alcohol and drug usage): _____

_____

_____

_____

_____

What is the role of the man in the relationship? What is the role of the woman in the relationship? _____

_____

_____

_____

_____

Style and manner of dress (e.g., wearing stockings or head coverings): _____

_____

_____

_____

_____

Rules that govern sex (before marriage and after marriage): _____

_____

_____

_____

_____

_____

Birth control: _____

_____

_____

_____

_____

_____

Holidays/traditions: _____

_____

_____

_____

_____

The Sabbath: _____

_____

_____

_____

_____

THE FUTURE

When you think about your relationship long-term, it is important to consider how your belief systems will manifest in your lives as a couple and family. For example, it can be easy to assume that your partner will automatically join you in your practices and traditions, but assumptions can lead to disappointments. Think about how you see your relationship ideally playing out and what expectations you have of yourself and your partner. Also consider room for growth and flexibility. You may have found in the earlier exercises that you have grown from some beliefs of your upbringing, and perhaps that may happen again as life progresses. Through time and with life's experiences, it is helpful to be open to the possibility for growth, questioning, and learning. The clearer and more detailed you are about your general vision and goals for the future, the more honest you can be with your partner and the more realistic your expectations of each other will become.

⊘ Now, for each topic, check the box that applies to you. Consider how you would like your partner and future family to fit into that vision and be sure to write out any additional notes you think of as you do this exercise. It will be important to describe to your partner your expectations and vision for your relationship and family.

Ideal Future Practices	Agree	Neutral	Disagree
I want us to attend worship services frequently.			
I want my partner to be involved in my spiritual practices.			
I want us to serve/volunteer in a faith-based capacity.			
I am open to reading/learning about more than one religious text (Bible, Qur'an, etc.).			
I want us to raise our children with a certain religious/spiritual/faith system. If you agree, name it here: _____.			
Certain holidays have religious importance to me.			
My partner and I can have different religious/spiritual beliefs.			
My partner and I can attend different faith communities/services.			
I believe that our children should be allowed to choose their own spiritual path.			
I want nature to be a part of our spiritual practices.			

Hopefully this list will be a foundational place for you and your partner to discuss where you align and where you differ. If you find that there are areas where you don't align, there still may be ways that you can complement each other. You may have similar underlying values that can serve as a connection. Think about ways you can be flexible and open with one another's varying beliefs.

After reviewing the "Ideal Future Practices" table above with your partner, identify areas of disagreement. For the areas where you do not align, think about whether there is room for flexibility or whether there are nonnegotiables. Continue to have discussions about how you will engage in spiritual practices as a couple.

As a result of your weekly discussion:

⬤ Our identified strengths in this area are: _____

_____

_____

_____

_____

_____

⬤ The things that we need to continue to talk about in this area are:

_____

_____

_____

_____

_____

⬤ What are your next steps? How will you work on your growth areas? Write down your plan of action. For example, will you seek help from others (i.e., a counselor, therapist, or mentor), or will you two read, study, and discuss together as a couple? _____

_____

_____

_____

_____

_____

Resources for further information on spiritual growth:

— *The Black Church: This Is Our Story, This Is Our Song* by Henry Louis Gates Jr. (2021).
— *5-Minute Couple's Devotional: 150 Days of Love, Reflection, and Prayer* by Jake Morrill (2021).

CHAPTER 3

His and Hers (Gender Roles)

*G*ender roles—a socially constructed term—describe socially acceptable behaviors, characteristics, and expectations commonly associated with being either male or female. These roles are often based on the specific society in which people live. We tend to think about gender roles in two ways: traditional and nontraditional. Traditional gender roles for men and women are primarily based on Western European standards. For example, men are strong, aggressive leaders and heads of the household; they are expected to be the breadwinners, ensuring all financial security for the family. Traditionally, "man's work" includes heavy lifting, taking out the trash, completing yard work, making repairs around the house, and taking care of the car. On the opposite end of the spectrum, women are "supposed to be" nurturing, soft caretakers of the home and take on all domestic duties, including caring for the children, cooking, and cleaning. *Egalitarian gender roles,*

a nontraditional approach, emphasize shared household, parenting, and financial re-sponsibilities. Egalitarian couples work as a team, navigating the needs and responsi-bilities of the home with flexibility instead of conforming to the rigid expectations of a traditional approach.

Historically, African men and women had no problem managing work life and home life. The African heritage, rich in family values, encouraged men and women to take great pride in navigating their separate roles to collectively support and provide for the family. However, Western European traditional gender roles have been incor-rectly and unfairly used as the standard for African American relationships. We know that historical, social, and economic factors made it virtually impossible for African American relationships to attain this standard of living.

The institution of slavery—plagued with racism, discrimination, and oppression—drastically changed and shaped the African American family and transformed the gender roles of African Americans. Enslaved men could not provide financially for their families, much less offer physical protection to their wives and children, be-cause doing so may have resulted in death. Enslaved women functioned as caregivers, cooking, cleaning, and raising the children of the white enslavers at the expense of their own children and family's well-being, while being forced to work in the fields alongside men. The gender roles that were once fulfilled with pride and honor became nonexistent. The enslaved women were considered "genderless" and expected to carry out the same hard labor as the men, according to Patricia Dixon in the book *African American Relationships, Marriages, and Families: An Introduction.*

After slavery, the inability of Black men to provide financially for their families forced Black women to enter the workforce while, in many instances, the men became caretakers of the home. In some ways, the Black woman's role was made masculine as she became the breadwinner for the family, and the Black man's role was made fem-inine in relation to traditional roles. *Racial discrimination*, oppression, and assumed gender roles were all factors that became the breeding ground for many stereotypes applied to and profoundly affecting African Americans today.

Stereotypes projected onto Black men include the idea that they are lazy and un-faithful, don't provide for their families, and, even worse, are weak and incompetent. Navigating these labels forced Black men to reconcile their idea of what it means to be a man. Many Black men grapple with the understanding that their manhood is tied to their ability to perform traditional gender roles based on Western European socially acceptable standards. Yet, they clearly have never been given the same fair opportunity as white men and therefore lack the resources to attain the socially defined traditional idea of manhood. In like fashion, Black women, having had to enter the workforce because of financial oppression and discrimination, have had to navigate the stereo-type of the strong Black woman who falsely bears the labels of being emasculating, aggressive, and controlling while, without feelings, being able to bear the weight of the world on her shoulders. The experience and belief of these negative stereotypes have shaped the Black experience and, unfortunately, continue to have an impact on African American relationships.

Differing ideas about gender roles can foster conflict in relationships, particularly if there are unrealistic or unspoken expectations. Each person enters the relationship with their own experiences and expectations often derived from society, cultural norms, tradition, and the family. From the legacy of enslavement came the idea that African American mothers "raise their daughters and love their sons." For the most part, African American daughters have been raised to be strong, responsible, and focused on their careers, to make sure that they can financially support themselves. This can often lead to behaviors that reflect the strong Black woman stereotype and can block the success of a relationship. She has been raised and socialized to believe that she is a "superwoman" and that "she does not need a man." Despite her desire for a loving, supportive, trustworthy, dependable, and financially responsible spouse, her experiences, her observations, and the messages passed down from other women in her family tell her otherwise. The idea of being vulnerable and relying on a man involves too much risk. Therefore, it is easier to maintain the stereotypical assumption that Black men are unreliable, unstable, and unable to provide the financial security she expects or hopes for. The unwillingness to be vulnerable leads to defensive, guarded behavior and subsequent isolation from her spouse.

Meanwhile, unemployment, low wages, and oppression have made it difficult for many Black men to attain traditional social status. When this lack of status, combined with the internalization of the negative stereotype of being weak and incompetent, is activated, a Black man feels defensive and emotionally unavailable. These stereotypes and the expectations of gender roles are automatically expressed in the relationship, resulting in power struggles that ultimately impede the couple's vulnerability and intimate emotional connection.

As with any relationship, healthy conflict resolution requires compromise and flexibility and should be based on current factors. For example, current circumstances may warrant one person taking on more responsibilities inside the home while the other person carries more responsibility outside the home. This decision may be influenced not just by finances but also by work schedule and flexibility. The husband may take the responsibility of getting children prepared and off to school as his schedule may permit, leaving the wife to pick them up after school and prepare dinner. Another critical concept is flexibility. Flexibility is a primary solution to conflicts. There may come a season in the marriage when there is a role reversal and a shift in responsibilities. The partner in the home who once carried the financial responsibility may no longer be able to do so, and the partner who had been at home may be thrust into the working world. As life changes, it is essential for the couple to engage in open dialogue and to communicate how to make adjustments.

African American families today utilize a more flexible approach to navigating family operations. Dual-income families require more flexibility in the sharing of household responsibilities. Hence, egalitarianism is a strength of the African American couple, instead of the traditional roles defined by a Western European culture imposed on Blacks. Don't allow your relationship to succumb to the opposing views and stereotypes formed by a European standard of what a real, healthy relationship should look like. You and your partner are encouraged to create roles and responsibilities in the marriage based solely on both of your current circumstances, capabilities, and desires. Examine one another's areas of strength and growth and then determine what responsibilities each will carry. Assess which partner is stronger at managing the finances. Which partner is better at cooking? For example, when discussing who will perform certain chores, don't overlook the option of considering a housekeeper, especially if you both work outside the home. Expectations of one another should factor in who is the most capable and how you can work together to achieve the desired goals for your household. We firmly believe that gender role ideals, gender role expectations, and the influence of the family of origin are essential factors for couples to explore and process. Equally important is a conversation or exploration about negative gendered stereotypes and how they may show up in the relationship. Understanding and insight gained through dialogue, compromise, and flexibility are essential to building a more harmonious relationship.

THE PAST

African American families have taken various forms as a result of American enslavement. The structure of the African American family ranges from single-parent households (headed by a woman or a man) to two-parent homes to multigenerational households with extended family and close friends who act like family. Depending on the family type, roles and responsibilities may vary. A two-parent household may function with one income and nontraditional roles: the woman is the breadwinner and the husband is the homemaker. The roles and responsibilities in a two-parent, dual-income household may look very different, as there may be shared responsibilities in childcare and household duties. Though egalitarian roles are a strength for most African American families, the traditional family roles of the husband operating as the breadwinner and the wife as the homemaker are also still present and most endorsed by society.

Regardless of the family structure in which you were raised, there is value in being aware of the roles and responsibilities you observed in your childhood home. Have you ever given some thought to your expectations around gender roles? The expectations you have of yourself and your partner are primarily informed by past experiences, and sometimes the unspoken expectations can be a significant source of contention. Awareness is key.

Take a minute and think about the roles you observed in your childhood home. Identify who performed the various tasks in your childhood home. Mark "M" for Mother, "F" for Father, "B" for both, or "N" for neither.

___ Did the cooking

___ Did laundry

___ Washed dishes

___ Did the driving

___ Transported children to school

___ Picked up children

___ Changed oil in vehicles

___ Helped children with homework/school projects

___ Bathed children before bed

___ Combed children's hair

___ Prepared school lunches

___ Did the housekeeping

___ Took time off work when children were sick

___ Managed the finances

___ Did the grocery shopping

___ Dried/put away dishes

___ Cleaned bathroom daily

___ Swept and mopped kitchen

___ Planned vacations

___ Did household repairs

___ Opened and sorted mail

___ Prepared taxes

___ Transported children to extracurricular activities

___ Paid the bills

___ Did yard work

___ Disciplined children

___ Scheduled and attended children's medical appointments

___ Vacuumed and dusted

___ Pumped gas

___ Planned social outings

___ Attended parent-teacher conferences

___ Made decisions for the family

___ Took out the trash

___ Washed vehicles

___ Provided spiritual leadership

 How would you describe the gender roles in your household? What were women responsible for? What were men responsible for? _____

_____

_____

_____

_____

_____

_____

 Complete the following statements:

I was raised to believe a wife should: _____

_____

_____

_____

_____

_____

◎ I was raised to believe a husband should: _____

_____

_____

_____

_____

_____

THE PRESENT

Given that past experiences often influence our present behaviors, it is vital for a couple to recognize and identify what behaviors and expectations they bring into the relationship and how they affect the relationship. Have you ever given any thought to how you move through your daily life? Have you ever really examined and questioned your behaviors? For example, do you operate in a more traditional gender role? If traditional gender roles were followed in your family, you may have naturally inherited the same beliefs. As a woman, maybe you enjoy cooking and cleaning. While there is nothing wrong with enjoying such tasks, have you ever asked yourself, "Why do I enjoy cooking and cleaning?" Is it because you love the feeling of stirring food and adding special spices, along with neatly folding warm clothes? Or could you have taken on the role because somehow you thought it was expected? As a man, do you enjoy taking out the trash, doing yard work, and following other traditionally male roles, or have you fallen into these roles because you were raised to believe it is what "a man" should do? Maybe you don't enjoy any of those things and carry guilt because you don't, or maybe others talk about you because you are not fulfilling your "duties" as a woman or man.

Perhaps you were raised in a two-parent home, and now you are a single parent navigating nontraditional gender roles. Regardless of the situation, have some awareness about how you are navigating your life around gender roles and what adjustments you are willing to make for your future marriage. How flexible are you regarding gender roles?

♡ As an adult, what roles have you taken on in relationships? Are they similar or dissimilar to those you were raised with? _____

_____

_____

_____

_____

_____

_____

_____

_____

⊙⊙ What expectations do you have of your partner in your current relationship
that you recognize came from your family of origin? _____
_____
_____
_____
_____

Check the response that best describes your belief about male and female roles in the
relationship. Compare your answers with your partner's and discuss the similarities
and differences.

	Strongly Agree	Agree	Neutral	Disagree	Strongly Disagree
The man is the head of the household.					
The woman should not work outside the home.					
Household chores should be shared.					
The man should discipline the children.					
The woman should keep the home clean.					
The woman should do the cooking.					
The man should always initiate sexual intimacy.					
Both the man and woman should discipline the children.					
Both the man and woman should be expected to have a job/paycheck.					
The man should take out the trash and do yard work.					
Children should be made to do chores.					
Children should receive allowances for good grades and chores.					

	Strongly Agree	Agree	Neutral	Disagree	Strongly Disagree
The man should handle the money.					
The man should have the final say on decisions.					
The man should pay all the bills.					
The woman's money is hers.					
The man should lead the family spiritually.					
The woman handles medical appointments.					
The woman handles school activities for the children.					

Did you become aware of any negative stereotypes about Black men and women that you've had? Have there been times when your behavior might have reinforced negative stereotypes in your relationship? If so, describe.

_____

_____

_____

_____

THE FUTURE

In couples, it is not uncommon for one partner to have been raised with traditional gender roles, while the other partner may have been raised in a single-parent or even a two-parent home in which the responsibilities and expectations differed. Neither is wrong: they are just different, and if not discussed, the differences can lead to significant conflict and disconnections. The idea is not to change the other person's expectations. Instead, discuss and examine the expectations related to gender roles in the relationship. Expectations are commonly based on how we want our partners to behave. In truth, they are frequently transferred onto our partners based on our past experiences, and conflict is likely to happen when the expectations are unrealistic or not agreed on.

Review your responses to the exercises from "The Past" and "The Present." Now think about your expectations and desires for your future marriage. Answer the following questions.

How do you envision gender roles in your future marriage (traditional/nontraditional)? Describe. _____

_____

_____

_____

_____

How will you decide who does what and who has responsibility for what in the marriage? Describe. _____

_____

_____

_____

_____

Take a moment to think about the specific tasks required to operate your future household, and *together* identify who will complete the following chores. Mark "M" for yourself, "P" for your partner, or "B" for both. Write down any additional items not included in this list.

___ Wash dishes
___ Clean bathroom daily
___ Do the cooking
___ Do the driving
___ Do laundry
___ Do yard work
___ Sweep and mop kitchen
___ Put away laundry
___ Plan vacations
___ Vacuum and dust
___ Wash vehicles/pump gas

___ Arrange for childcare
___ Take out the trash
___ Do the grocery shopping
___ Plan social outings
___ Provide spiritual leadership
___ Help children with homework
___ Manage medical appointments
___ Manage the finances
___ Dry/put away dishes
___ Attend parent-teacher conferences

How will you continue to reassess your roles and responsibilities during the life of your relationship? Describe. _____

_____

_____

_____

_____

Gender roles should not be assumed, as they can vary depending on the relationship. Whether you identify with traditional or nontraditional gender roles, they should be flexible. You are encouraged to examine what expectations around gender roles you bring into the relationship and to be aware of what you desire in your future relationship. Differences should be explored, discussed, and agreed on based on the strengths, desires, and capabilities of both you and your partner. Make sure you are not harboring unrealistic expectations, stereotypes, or anything that will likely result in conflict. If peace is the goal, then engage in ongoing flexible discussions and be willing to renegotiate and adjust to life changes.

Take some time to think about your areas of strength and your growth areas and how you plan to address them. You might find that you cannot address these challenges in a productive way that is beneficial to the relationship. If this is the case, consider exercising the strength to seek the help of a professional therapist to assist you and your partner.

As a result of your weekly discussion:

Our identified strengths in this area are: _____

_____

_____

_____

_____

_____

The things that we need to continue to talk about in this area are:

_____

_____

_____

_____

_____

What are your next steps? How will you work on your growth areas? Write down your plan of action. For example, will you seek help from others (i.e., a counselor, therapist, or mentor), or will you two read, study, and discuss together as a couple? _____

_____

_____

_____

_____

Resources for further information on gender roles:

- *Sharing Chores: Effective Ways to Share Household Chores in Marriage* (Kindle Edition) by Dr. Washington (2022).
- *The Fair Play Deck: A Couple's Conversation Deck for Prioritizing What's Important* by Eve Rodsky (2020).

CHAPTER 4

He Said, She Said (Communication)

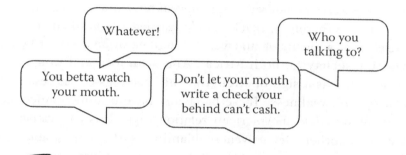

ommunication is necessary in any relationship. Communication must be effective in everyday interactions, as well as in resolving conflict. *Effective communication* is fundamental to the sustainability of a healthy relationship. *Merriam-Webster* defines communication as "a process by which information is exchanged between individuals through a common system of symbols, signs, or behavior." There is a giving and receiving of thoughts, an expression of emotion, and the sending of messages. All communication requires a sender and a receiver, a talker and a listener. Essentially, communication is a process of understanding and sharing meaning. This sharing occurs in many forms.

Communication experts have found that 7 percent of communication is based on verbal content (*what* we say); 38 percent is based on tone and pitch (*how* we speak); and the remaining 55 percent is based on body language, facial expressions, hand gestures, and eye movement. These verbal and nonverbal behaviors construct messages. However, tone and nonverbal behavior convey the "heart" of the message. Harmony between what is said, what is felt, and what is displayed is the goal of effective communication. For example, if you smack your lips, roll your eyes, and cross your arms while saying, "I'm good, we cool," communication is not effective. Communication in intimate relationships requires two fundamental elements: *emotional awareness* and *emotional vulnerability*. Emotional awareness is the ability to accurately identify current feelings and internal states. Emotional vulnerability is the ability and willingness to share these feelings with your partner.

Throughout American history, Black people were not afforded the luxury of expressing their emotions and vulnerability. Emotions and vulnerability were not safe, because they were considered a sign of weakness and could be used to exploit, threaten, or coerce. Therefore, Black people learned to guard their emotions and shield themselves as a means of survival. A tough emotional armor became essential to navigating society for both African American men and women: displays of anger were accepted as a sign of strength, while feelings of sadness or hurt were avoided as a sign of weakness. These behaviors have become embedded into the framework of many African American relationships. This can cause partners to turn against one another. Defensiveness, blaming, withdrawing, and being highly critical of one another can become the central theme of interactions, often fueled by a lack of respect, trust, and even safety. We find that these couples have a genuine desire to connect on an intimately emotional level. Still, this process is often thwarted or impaired by how the couple has learned to engage and talk to one another.

True communication is considered an intimate act, and both people in the relationship must be emotionally available and vulnerable enough to ask for what they need. Many couples struggle to be emotionally vulnerable and often have difficulty asking for what they "really" need. In some cases, the mere thought of asking for what they need is not an option. In the absence of emotional vulnerability and availability, couples often resort to *unhealthy communication* strategies as an alternative, which proves to be unproductive and, in most instances, damaging to the relationship. Unhealthy communication often involves the sender/talker using blaming and unclear messages and the receiver/listener listening to respond rather than listening to hear/understand. We believe healthy, successful relationships are not perfect relationships. A healthy relationship involves insight into communication styles, defensive patterns, and the influence of the family. We encourage couples to examine their interactions and utilize tools that will enhance their communication.

Effective Communication

Effective Sender/Talker	Effective Receiver/Listener
Use "I" statements (avoid "you" statements).	Listen with an open heart and mind.
Be gentle (no one wants to hear how they messed up).	Don't immediately defend your position.
Be aware of your emotional temperature (too hot or too cold can cloud the message).	Repeat what you heard them say and confirm you heard right (ask for clarification).
Be direct and stay on one topic.	Seek to understand first and then seek to be understood.
Slow down.	Minimize distractions/give your full attention.
Remember that you are allies, not enemies.	Remember that you are allies, not enemies.
Say how you feel and what you need.	Don't make it about you (until the talker has finished their points).
Ask for a time-out if things get heated.	Ask for a time-out if things get heated.

THE PAST

Our communication styles are rooted in or informed by what we observed and experienced in our homes while growing up. Our families influence how we learn to share our thoughts, feelings, and wants and how we interact with others in the world. The concept of open communication may have been discouraged for some, particularly in Black families. The basis for open communication is represented by a space to speak freely and express emotions. For some families, this was frowned upon, as it was often interpreted as disrespectfully "talking back." Perhaps communication in your family was demonstrated through raised voices, yelling, or cursing. In some families, the tone was the same whether you were speaking in love or you were in trouble. Maybe you came from a big family where *active listening* was foreign, as everyone spoke loudly and over one another just to be heard. Or you may have observed hostile, angry verbal exchanges riddled with name-calling and disrespect. Communication in your family while you were growing up may have involved shutting down and keeping your thoughts and emotions bottled up: in many households, it was understood that children were to be seen and not heard. Believe it or not, silence can become the language of the family. Regardless of how we observed and learned to communicate in our families, there were implied messages in the meaning making that occurred.

We believe that before you can know where you are going, you must know where you were. To understand our current behavior patterns and communication styles, we must go back to where it all began.

Five Communication Styles

1. *Passive*—A person communicating in a passive style does not say what they are thinking or feeling. The passive person acts like they don't care about the outcome or decision that needs to be made. They tend to agree with whatever the other person wants and doesn't share their wants and needs. They may say, "I'm fine either way" or "I'll let you decide."

2. *Aggressive*—A person communicating in an aggressive style expresses their feelings in a way that violates others. The goal of aggressive communication is to dominate and "win," even at the other's expense. They may use intimidation, insults, criticism, or sarcasm to get their point across. They may say, "I said what I said," "You sound real stupid right now," or "This is how it is and that's it."

3. *Passive-aggressive*—A person communicating in a passive-aggressive style uses hidden forms of aggression to express their feelings. They often seem passive at first but act out their "anger" or disapproval in indirect and subtle ways. They may use body language or behavior to express their thoughts and feelings. However, those may be the opposite of what they say. They may say, "We're cool," but stop talking to you for a week.

4. *Submissive*—The submissive person gives in to others' demands, requests, or feelings. They also don't acknowledge their own concerns, feelings, or wants. When they do, it is usually in a timid/apologetic way. Sadly, they are often ignored. People who communicate submissively try to avoid conflict at all costs and want to play it safe while putting others' needs first. They may say, "Whatever you like," "Whatever you want," or "Whatever you think is best."

5. *Assertive (the ideal way to communicate)*—A person communicating assertively expresses thoughts and feelings directly and honestly. They stand up for their personal rights and give direct messages in appropriate ways. Assertive communication gives the message that the feelings and needs of both people are important. They say, "I get sad when I don't hear from you all day. Can you at least text during lunch to say hi, babe."

The goal is to be an assertive communicator.

 Look at the five communication styles above and then, in the table below, write down the communication style used most by those closest to you while you were growing up. If you have multiple people in a category, just use the same box for them all (e.g., the styles for both grandmothers can be in the same box; the styles for all brothers can go in the "Brothers" box).

Family Member	Communication Style
Mother (stepmother)	
Father (stepfather)	
Grandmother	
Grandfather	
Aunts	
Uncles	
Brothers	
Sisters	
Others:	
Others:	

Take a minute to reflect on how you learned to communicate in your family. Then answer the following questions.

How would you describe communication in your family while you were growing up? _____ _____ _____ _____ _____ _____ _____

Between the adults? _____ _____ _____ _____ _____ _____

Between the children and the adults? _____ _____ _____ _____ _____ _____

Describe the communication styles between you and your siblings, you and your friends, and you and your other family members while you were growing up. _____

_____

_____

_____

_____

_____

_____

_____

_____

_____

_____

_____

_____

How was love, approval, and validation expressed in your family while you were growing up? _____

_____

_____

_____

_____

_____

_____

_____

_____

_____

_____

_____

_____

How was conflict and disapproval expressed in your family while you were growing up? _____

_____

_____

_____

_____

_____

_____

_____

_____

_____

_____

_____

How did you feel after communicating important information to adults when you were a child? Check the boxes that describe communication in your childhood home. Check all that apply.

☐ I felt heard.
☐ I felt seen.
☐ I felt like it wasn't okay to express emotions in my household.

☐ I felt like "What's the point?"
☐ I felt misunderstood.
☐ I felt better.
☐ I felt worse.
☐ I felt scared.

How you felt after having difficult conversations in your family while you were growing up might affect how safe you feel sharing in your current relationship. Vulnerability can be scary for many long into adulthood. The good news is that healthy communication in your current relationship can help repair the wounds of childhood. Begin by letting your partner know what communication meant to you as a child and work together to create the safety needed to move forward.

THE PRESENT

The words we choose to get our points across can have lasting effects, particularly in intimate relationships. It has been said that people don't remember what you say to them: instead, they remember how you make them feel. Words have meaning, and powerful words can lift and illuminate, or they can destroy and tear down your partner. Words are like bullets; once they are launched or spoken, they can't be taken back or unheard. The emotional damage and impact of hurtful words can ultimately lead to the destruction of the relationship. Thus, choose your words wisely, and think about how you deliver the message.

The communication patterns observed in our work can be described from various perspectives. One perspective is offered by Drs. John and Julie Schwartz Gottman, leading research experts on couples conflict. The Gottmans remind us that even the healthiest relationships have conflict. They maintain that the key is knowing how to address the conflict. The Gottmans identify four communication types that are *not* effective and can prove damaging to the relationship. Known as the *Four Horsemen of the Apocalypse*, these strategies, particularly if they persist or go unbridled, will undoubtedly lead to the demise of the relationship.

The components of the Four Horsemen include:

1. *Criticism*—Blaming or attacking your partner's character, personality, or motives. This usually includes statements like "You just like your mama" or "You always trippin'."

2. *Defensiveness*—Denying, minimizing, blaming, or failing to take responsibility for one's behavior. It invalidates the partner and usually begins with a counterargument: "You trippin'!" "Yeah, but what about when you . . ." "I don't do that." "Get over it, that was a long time ago."

3. *Contempt*—Involves sarcasm, ridicule, and name-calling. The partner often displays feelings of disgust and disrespect toward the other. Contempt is the most toxic and has a high likelihood of leading to divorce: "You make me sick, I can't stand you." "You ain't nothing but a . . ." "Why can't you be like . . ."

4. *Stonewalling*—Withdrawing, ignoring, or avoiding the partner and refusing to acknowledge their point of view. Stonewalling is different from taking time-out to calm down. The goal of a time-out is to cool off, with the intention of coming back together to discuss the problem when you are both calm. In stonewalling, the person shuts down and has no desire to discuss the particular issue at any point in time. They make no room to work out the issue. Examples are "I'm good" or "I'll be back" and short answers like "yep," "no," or "I don't know."

Although couples may find themselves engaging in these negative behaviors that have been proven to be poisonous to a relationship, the good news is that there is hope. This hope is called the *antidote*, which means medicine or remedy. Couples can move away from the painful, destructive behaviors of the Four Horsemen to more positive interactions that strengthen the relationship, causing each person to feel close, validated, and supported. The best way to cure or reduce the effect of the Four Horsemen in your relationship is to apply the following antidotes:

1. *The antidote for criticism: gentle start-up*—Make a comment that focuses on specific behavior and what you need, instead of criticizing or attacking your partner's character or suggesting they are flawed. Ask yourself, "What do I feel?" and "What do I need?" You want to stay away from saying words like "you always" or "you never," as these tend to put the other person on the defensive. Instead, use "I" statements to express your need. An example of a gentle start-up to express a complaint is: "Babe, I feel disappointed to see you watching television while I am cooking and trying to do laundry. I could really use your help right now." The opposite would be: "Why are you just sitting there chilling while I'm taking care of all the housework? I worked all day too."

2. *The antidote for defensiveness: take responsibility*—It is natural to want to defend yourself when you feel you are being criticized or attacked. But we know defensiveness is never helpful. Control the natural tendency to go on the defense when your partner presents a complaint. Instead, start by taking responsibility for the behavior or ownership for a part of the problem.

For example, look at the above complaint about not helping around the house. Instead of saying, "Man, whatever," it might be helpful to respond with, "I know you worked all day. My bad. What can I help you with?" Sometimes, a simple acknowledgment and taking responsibility are the best ways to quickly bring peace to a situation.

3. *The antidote for contempt: build a culture of appreciation and respect*—You can change the entire atmosphere of your relationship by looking for and expressing the good in your partner, instead of focusing on what they do that you do not like. Simply put, stop focusing on what your partner is doing "wrong" and shift your focus to what he or she is doing right. Look for opportunities to regularly express appreciation and gratitude for your partner. For example, think of two or three things about your partner's personality that you like or are thankful for and why. Just by sharing this with them, you have begun to change the atmosphere in the relationship.

   Another way to begin to cure contempt is to use the five-to-one ratio (one of our favorites). This means that for every one negative interaction with your partner, there needs to be five positive interactions. This may include sending a sweet text; leaving a love note; or offering some other gesture of kindness and affection, such as a hug or kiss. This might be difficult at the beginning, so try starting with a three-to-one ratio.

4. *The antidote for stonewalling: self-soothing/comforting yourself*—When one partner engages in stonewalling, it is usually to remove themselves emotionally and, sometimes, physically. The emotions can be so overwhelming that the person's heart begins to race and their palms sweat. These are the body's response to the pressure. It is as if the body is sending an alarm that says, "This is too much" and "I need to get out of here." Gottman suggests self-soothing as a remedy. The first step is to recognize that you need to take a break so that you can calm down and return to the conversation with positive behaviors. You might consider expressing to your partner, "Sweetheart, I am having a hard time right now, and I am feeling emotionally overwhelmed. Can I have about twenty minutes to get myself together and come back so we can talk?" This also lets your partner know that you intend to return to the conversation. During your time-out, engage in activities that are soothing and distracting for a brief period. Examples include listening to music, exercising, drawing, or whatever activity you might enjoy that will help you to relax and calm down and allow you to be emotionally present with your partner. The goal is to calm down so that you can continue to work through the issue.

If any of the Four Horsemen make an appearance in your relationship, consider the antidote for treatment. Be vigilant and always ready to attack the Horsemen, not one another.

Now let's examine your current communication style and how well you and your partner communicate. Look back at the five communication styles in the section "The Past."

How would you describe your communication style? _____

_____

_____

_____

_____

_____

_____

_____

_____

_____

Describe your partner's communication style. _____

_____

_____

_____

_____

_____

_____

_____

_____

Do you notice any similarities or differences in the way your family communicated compared to how you currently communicate? How do you believe the communication style of your family of origin influences your own style? _____

_____

_____

_____

_____

_____

_____

_____

Read the following definitions and mark the communication type that best describes *your* behavior when there is a conflict with your partner. You can choose more than one.

☐ Criticism—I become critical of my partner.
☐ Defensiveness—I feel attacked and immediately turn the tables.
☐ Contempt—I engage in sarcasm, mocking, and name-calling.
☐ Stonewalling—I shut down and walk away.
☐ Other

Read the following definitions and mark the communication type that best describes your *partner* when there is a conflict. You can choose more than one.

☐ Criticism—They become critical of me.
☐ Defensiveness—They feel attacked and immediately turn the tables.
☐ Contempt—They engage in sarcasm, mocking, and name-calling.
☐ Stonewalling—They shut down and shut me out.
☐ Other

Which antidotes to the Four Horsemen would you like to incorporate into your relationship? Write a plan on how you can do so. _____

_____

_____

_____

_____

_____

_____

_____

_____

_____

_____

_____

_____

_____

_____

_____

_____

_____

Using "I" statements and avoiding criticism, defensiveness, contempt, and stonewalling in your communication will lay a foundation for developing healthy and productive
interactions with your partner. These strategies will get you and your partner closer to
creating the relationship you desire.

   Think about a time when you and your partner did not communicate well.
Let's practice using "I" statements. Complete the sentence below using your
feelings at that time, the behavior you didn't like, and what you needed
instead.

I feel _____ (insert feeling) when you _____
_____ (insert specific statement or behavior); what I need
from you is _____ (insert specific
behavior or alternative response).

Remember to continue to practice using "I" statements when communicating your
needs, desires, frustrations, and hurts to your partner. This can go a long way! Another
chance to practice is in appendix B.

THE FUTURE

The quality of a relationship is often dictated by how well you can effectively communicate with your partner. We encourage you to think about your communication style
and note how you engage in disagreements. Is it effective? In preparation for building
a future together, you must communicate about communication. Prepare to discuss
what you want the communication style to look like in your future family. What will
be the rules of engagement between you two? What about children and communication: How much freedom of expression will the children be given? These can be
challenging but necessary conversations, especially if you and your partner have very
different childhood experiences with family communication.

Equally important are the guidelines for how you and your spouse will manage
conflict or argue in front of the children. You might be adamant about not allowing
the children to know there is trouble in paradise, and your partner may not care. We
strongly encourage you as a couple to consider the impact of how you navigate disagreements and what you want to model for your children.

However, you and your partner may decide not to have children. Even so, you must
discuss boundaries around communication between the two of you. For example, you
might set a rule that there will be no arguing via text or email. You might send an
emoji expressing frustration via text, but you can agree that heavy, serious discussions should not be addressed with technology. This type of behavior can be seen as

passive-aggressive and, in most cases, will not lead to either person getting what they desire. When discussions become too heated, have a plan for how you will pause and take a time-out when needed. You both might consider an agreed-on code word that signals it's time to take a break. Additionally, have discussions about what information is shared outside of the house. You might have been raised with the common family rule, "What goes on in this house stays in this house," or you might be from the "I tell my mama everything" group. Either way, there should be a discussion to find a balance that you both can agree on.

As you and your partner navigate various communication topics, keep in mind how you currently communicate and your desired future communication style. The goal is to foster an environment where healthy, effective communication can occur for everyone.

Think about your future marriage and answer the following questions.

How might your style of communication be helpful or harmful to your partner? _____

_____

_____

_____

_____

_____

_____

How would you like to communicate with your partner? How would you like your partner to communicate with you? _____

_____

_____

_____

_____

_____

What area of communication would you like to work on to ensure that you maintain a healthy relationship? _____

_____

_____

_____

_____

_____

◎ What changes are you willing to make to ensure that you have a deep emotional connection with your partner? _____

_____

_____

_____

_____

_____

_____

_____

Effective communication is vital to healthy relationships. Healthy relationships involve communication that allows sharing thoughts and feelings in a way that is received, acknowledged, and understood. Recognition and insight into your own communication style, defensive behaviors, and family influences are a great way to minimize misunderstandings and reduce potential conflicts. Another critical aspect of healthy communication is an emotional connection built on a foundation of safety. We encourage you to continue to foster a safe environment where each person can engage in emotional awareness, vulnerability, and transparency. Continue to utilize the tools that will enhance and not destroy your relationship. Be mindful of the words you use. Speak love and truth into your relationship. Don't ever stop talking. Instead of avoiding difficult conversations, create healthy boundaries and rules of engagement for more serious discussions. A great example would be to avoid using words like "never" and "always" because they are rarely ever true. One final helpful suggestion is to communicate to understand, not to be understood. Likewise, listen to understand, not to be understood.

Remember that in your best effort, you may still find it difficult to engage in healthy communication on your own. Know that it is more than okay to seek the help of a licensed professional to assist you with your communication journey. It is highly recommended.

As a result of your weekly discussion:

◎ Our identified strengths in this area are: _____

_____

_____

_____

_____

_____

⚭ The things that we need to continue to talk about in this area are: _____

_____
_____
_____
_____
_____

⚭ What are your next steps? How will you work on your growth areas? Write down your plan of action. For example, will you seek help from others (i.e., a counselor, therapist, or mentor), or will you two read, study, and discuss together as a couple? _____

_____
_____
_____
_____
_____

Resources for further information on communication:

— *Ten Lessons to Transform Your Marriage: America's Love Lab Experts Share Their Strategies for Strengthening Your Relationship* by John M. Gottman, Julie Schwartz Gottman, and Joan DeClaire (2007).
— *Love More, Fight Less: Communication Skills Every Couple Needs: A Relationship Workbook for Couples* by Gina Senarighi (2020).
— *Getting the Love You Want: A Guide for Couples* (Third Edition) by Harville Hendrix and Helen LaKelly Hunt (2019).

CHAPTER 5

Money Matters (Finances)

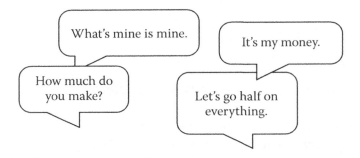

In essence, money matters—that is, conflicts about finances—are one of the leading causes of divorce, regardless of race. Though a lack of finances can present significant marital challenges, *how* the money is managed and who manages it are often at the center of conflict. However, examining other issues that lead to financial conflicts, such as different backgrounds and experiences with money, values, spending habits, and money-management skills, is essential and may help you avoid this pitfall.

The history of *systemic and institutionalized racism* and discrimination has left a stain on African American relationships/marriages. While American enslavement has had an impact on Black relationships in several ways, it has led to an outright assault on a couple's financial stability. American enslavement transformed traditional gender roles and robbed African American men of their ability to provide financially for their families. Even after enslavement, Black men and women continued to suffer. The effects of oppression and *marginalization* of Black men and women in the workforce, coupled with the lack of access to education, created severe challenges to the African American family. The long-term impact resulted in women becoming the working force for many families. The dynamic of the couple is significantly different from that of our white counterparts, as a Black woman is more likely to earn more than her partner and have more formal education. Moreover, African Americans may also face racial discrimination in the workplace, preventing advancement. Even with high achievement, the glass ceiling soon reminds us that we still have "limits." The economic and educational disadvantages result in a lack of access to resources, which can significantly impair the ability of African American families to attain wealth. Given that African Americans have higher rates of poverty compared to many other groups and that employment income for African Americans is significantly lower than that of whites, regardless of the level of education, it comes as no surprise that financial insecurity is cited as a dominant source of anxiety for African American men. While economic struggles are common in relationships, the above-mentioned factors can render African American couples more vulnerable to financial insecurity, yielding lasting effects and threats.

Although a lack of financial resources can put a strain on any relationship, conflict can also result from the couple entering the relationship with opposing ideas and beliefs about money and spending habits. Values about money vary from person to person. Nevertheless, these values and beliefs are often influenced by our past experiences with money, our family of origin's relationship with money, friends, and even religion. The financial resources available to your family can also help shape your worldview, attitudes, and expectations about money. Maybe your family was considered "poor" when you were growing up and money was tight; therefore, your family was extremely cautious with how money was spent. These experiences can either motivate you to repeat the same behavior, despite your financial success, or encourage you to throw caution to the wind and become carefree about buying whatever you desire. Meanwhile, your mate, raised in a home where money was not an issue, appears to be less cautious with money and finds no need for a budget. Two people coming together with different values about money are bound to generate conflict, especially if there is no discussion of or agreement on finances.

In our work with couples dealing with money matters, an exploration of behavior has often revealed that many women tend to follow the advice of older women who encourage a "just in case" fund. This money is secretly put aside "just in case" the marriage doesn't work out. This type of behavior can damage the marriage before it even gets started, by the woman entering the marriage with one foot already out the back door—not to mention the lying and secrecy needed to hide the funds, creating an environment of dishonesty. Spending habits can also create tension in your marriage. If you are a shopaholic, living paycheck to paycheck while incurring debt, and your spouse is a money miser, refusing to spend any money, conflict is inevitable. These contradicting money styles are a cocktail for divorce. Financial secrecy and lack of transparency are perhaps the most harmful to relationships. One partner may not reveal all their earnings and debt, thereby leaving the spouse blindsided and creating trust issues.

Regardless of the scenario, we encourage couples not to avoid having difficult conversations about money. Discuss attitudes, beliefs, and spending habits. We encourage you to consider *financial transparency* with your potential mate and to explore the meaning of money, to avoid major conflict or financial disaster.

THE PAST

Our attitudes and beliefs about money and our spending habits are often informed by our family of origin. Our financial understanding—or the lack of it—is also influenced by the financial behaviors of our caretakers. The distrust of financial institutions forced many Black people into different "saving" habits. Maybe your parents adopted the "mattress ministry," where they saved money under the mattress or in a sock drawer, and they were careful to save for rainy days. Maybe you were raised in a home where money was a sensitive topic, and the discussion of money rarely occurred. Or maybe you were raised in an affluent family where money was no object.

Take a moment to think about how the issue of money was addressed in your household when you were growing up and answer the following questions. Review your responses with your partner to jump-start the conversation about finances.

Identify your family of origin's financial status. Mark one.

- ☐ Money was never an issue. All my needs and wants were always met.
- ☐ Needs were always met. My desires were met most of the time.
- ☐ Money was an issue sometimes, but the needs were met.
- ☐ Money was always an issue, and it was hard to make ends meet.

Who handled the money in your family of origin? _____

Identify the responses that best describe your parent(s)'/caregiver(s)' relationship with money. Use "M" for Mother and "F" for Father. Mark all that apply.

___ Was not responsible with money.	___ Placed extremely high value on money.
___ Was very responsible with money.	
___ Worried a lot about money.	___ Was big on saving for a rainy day.
___ Was very nonchalant about money.	___ Was not good with saving money.

___ Did not deal with money.
___ Controlled all the money.
___ Created a lot of debt.
___ Spent too much money.
___ Was a big penny-pincher.
___ Had a positive/balanced
relationship with money.

___ Was too relaxed with money.
___ Was very strict with the budget.
___ Always went over the budget.
___ Lived off what they made, no
matter how much.
___ Always went to others for money.

THE PRESENT

Our current attitudes about money and spending habits can serve as a benefit or an obstacle in our relationships. The meaning and value we give to money may dictate financial success or failure. What money represents varies from person to person. For some, money means power, status, and control. The belief can be that money will equate to social acceptance, and therefore, money is used to manipulate and control others. For others, money represents security and independence; the more money you have, the more stable and secure your life will be. You have the freedom to do whatever you desire. While there may be some truth in this idea, you mustn't develop a false sense of security around money.

Is your image, self-esteem, and self-worth tied to money and materialism? It is imperative to assess the spending habits and money-management skills of you and your partner. Do you save your money, or are you living above your means in "trying to keep up with the Joneses"? Examine your own relationship to money, as it will have an impact on your future family life. Consider how you are spending your money. How honest are you willing to be with yourself and your partner about your current debt? These are questions to consider when trying to avoid the financial pitfalls experienced in many relationships.

In addition to these essential questions, answer the questions below.

How would you describe your current relationship with money? _____
_____
_____
_____
_____
_____
_____
_____
_____
_____

What is your partner's relationship with money as you see it? _____

_____

_____

_____

_____

_____

_____

_____

_____

_____

Use this scale to rate your attitude about finances.

	Definitely True	Somewhat True	Somewhat Not True	Definitely Not True
I consider myself to be financially responsible.				
I can take care of my monthly bills without the support of anyone else.				
I have asked others for financial help in the past six months.				
I struggle with managing my money.				
I don't have any concerns about the amount of money I make.				
Money is not an issue for me. I have plenty.				
I need more income to afford my current lifestyle.				
I live comfortably within my means.				
I contribute to saving money regularly.				
I sit down to do a budget monthly.				
Currently, I live paycheck to paycheck.				
I believe that if I earn it, I should be able to spend it how I choose to, and I do.				

Write down what concerns you have about money. Are there any behaviors or attitudes you would like to change? _____

_____

_____

_____

_____

_____

_____

_____

_____

_____

_____

_____

THE FUTURE

Financial security and wealth can be viewed as a desired goal for most, if not all, couples. Unfortunately, many obstacles interfere with these goals coming to fruition for African Americans. For some, the terms financial security and wealth are foreign concepts. The attitudes, beliefs, value systems about money, and spending habits learned in the family of origin make it difficult to achieve those goals. Perhaps this was your situation. We know that our past experiences with money can affect our current and future behaviors regarding money. It is also likely that you gained financial knowledge throughout your adulthood, adopted a new mindset, and learned different behaviors regarding money matters. Therefore, you can now make informed decisions about your future financial behaviors in your marriage. Now it's time to think about what this financial piece will look like. This is uncharted territory for some of you, and it can be a little scary. We encourage you and your partner to be courageous and engage in the process of exploring your finances and all that it entails. Hopefully, by now, you both have decided to be transparent about your finances, and now you can begin your marriage with mutually shared goals and dreams for your future together.

We encourage you to make decisions based on who is best suited to handle tasks and not based on past experiences. Open communication about your financial goals and investments is a recipe for success.

As you begin to prepare for your financial future together, take a moment to examine your ideas and beliefs about financial earnings in relation to gender. Society has a lot of messages about money and power, men and women. Many men are taught that their masculinity is based on how much money they make, and many Black women are taught that a man who doesn't make much money has no power in the household. These beliefs, if rigidly held, can be toxic and doom the relationship to failure.

Rate the following responses.

	Strongly Agree	Agree	Neutral	Disagree	Strongly Disagree
As a wife, I am okay with making a lot more money than my husband.					
As a husband, I am okay if my wife earns substantially more money than me.					
I will work more than one job to match my wife's income.					
My wife's income should be considered "extra."					
The husband should pay all the major bills in the household.					
The wife should take care of expenses for the children.					
All major purchases (e.g., $500 or more) should be discussed.					
All the money we make is considered household money.					
We both should have monthly allowances.					

Choose the response that matches how you would like money to be held or maintained.

☐ We should have separate accounts.
☐ Our money should be together in joint accounts.
☐ We should each have a separate account as well as a combined household account.
☐ Other

Who would you like to handle the finances and why? _____

_____

_____

_____

_____

_____

_____

_____

Take some time to think about your desired financial goals. Use the table below to list the goals you would like to achieve *immediately*, in *5–10 years*, and in *10–20 years*. Compare your list with your partner's and identify the *mutual* goals between you and your partner.

Financial Goals	IMMEDIATE	5–10 YEARS	10–20 YEARS
ME			
Income			
Savings			
Debt			
Investments			
Retirement Fund			
Homeownership			
PARTNER			
Income			
Savings			
Debt			
Investments			
Retirement Fund			
Homeownership			

Notes for discussion: _____

_____

_____

_____

_____

_____

_____

_____

_____

_____

_____

_____

Successful financial planning requires taking the first step: creating a budget. The process of establishing a budget requires knowing what you owe and what you own. Make a list of your monthly household income and expenses. Then schedule a time for you and your partner to come together as a couple and complete the combined column. Use the notes column to identify items that require future discussion.

INCOME (Gross)	ME	PARTNER	COMBINED	NOTES
Weekly				
Biweekly				
Monthly				
Medical Insurance				
Retirement				
Wage Garnishment				
TOTAL INCOME				

My Credit Score _____

(Choose one: TransUnion, Equifax, Experian)

EXPENSES	ME	PARTNER	COMBINED	NOTES
Housing				
Mortgage/Rent				
Utilities				
Phone				
Electricity				
Gas				
Water				
Cable				
Internet				
Cell Phone				
Other				
Transportation				
Car Note				
Insurance				
Gasoline				
Maintenance				
Other Transportation				
Food				
Groceries				
Eating Out				
Medical				
Doctor Visits				
Medication				
Other				
Children				
Tuition				
Childcare				
Child Support				
Activities				
Other				
Entertainment				
Outside				

EXPENSES	ME	PARTNER	COMBINED	NOTES
Hobbies				
Miscellaneous				
Personal				
Hair				
Nails/Feet				
Barber				
Dry Cleaning				
Other				
Credit and Loans				
Credit Cards				
Student Loans				
Personal Loans				
Life Insurance				
Memberships				
Donations				
Other				
Other				
Other				
Other				
TOTAL EXPENSES				

	ME	PARTNER	COMBINED	NOTES
TOTAL INCOME				
(Less Total Expenses)				
TOTAL REMAINING				

By completing this chapter, you have officially begun the journey of building your financial future. The hope is for you to have a sharpened sense of awareness about your values, attitudes, and beliefs about your finances. You are more aware of your spending habits, money-management skills, and financial growth areas. Moreover, you and your partner have a clear picture of your financial position and your future goals and dreams. May you continue to build on these recipes for success.

———————————————

As a result of your weekly discussion:

◎ Our identified strengths in this area are: _____

_____

_____

_____

_____

_____

◎ The things that we need to continue to talk about in this area are: _____

_____

_____

_____

_____

_____

◎ What are your next steps? How will you work on your growth areas? Write down your plan of action. For example, will you seek help from others (i.e., a counselor, therapist, or mentor), or will you two read, study, and discuss together as a couple? _____

_____

_____

_____

_____

_____

Resources for further information on financial management:

- *The Couple's Guide to Financial Compatibility: Avoid Fights About Spending and Saving—and Build a Happy and Secure Future Together* by Jeff Motske (2015).
- *Money Talks: The Ultimate Couple's Guide to Communicating About Money* by Talaat and Tai McNeely (2015).
- *The Black Financial Literacy and Wealth Building Bible: For Individual, Family and Community Empowerment* by David W. Fontaine (2019).

CHAPTER 6

*Blended
(Dating with Children)*

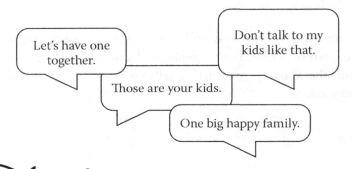

This chapter is dedicated to exploring ideas about *blended families*, so it may or may not be relevant to your relationship. But even if neither of you is bringing biological children into the relationship, it is beneficial to spend time thinking about your relationships and connections to any ex-partner's children or your family members' children for whom you have responsibilities. How might they be integrated into your marriage? Begin by answering the questions below and then discuss them with your partner.

Do you have continuing relationships with an ex-partner's children who are not biologically yours? If so, list the name(s) of your ex-partner(s) and the names and ages of the children.

Name of Ex-partner	Years Dated	Previously Lived Together	Name and age of children for whom you continue to care or with whom you have a relationship (e.g., buy birthday gifts, text/call, see)
1.		Yes No	1. 2. 3.
2.		Yes No	1. 2. 3.

 Has your partner continued relationships with an ex-partner's children who are not biologically theirs?   ☐Yes   ☐No

 How do you feel about the idea of your partner continuing to care for an ex-partner's children emotionally, financially, or physically (e.g., visitation and celebrations)? _____

_____

_____

_____

_____

_____

 Have you taken on a parental role with any other children who are not biologically related? When answering this question, think about any child you might have to "take in" if something happened to their parents (e.g., godchildren, a relative's children, a close friend's children). Name the children and describe your relationship with them: _____

_____

_____

_____

_____

_____

_____

Review your answers together. If none of the above applies to your relationship, and neither of you is bringing biological children into the relationship, you may choose to skip directly to chapter 7.

DEFINING THE FAMILY

Over the years, the definition, structure, and makeup of the family system have shifted significantly. In the not so distant past, the traditional marriage and family system were the aspirational norm. However, in this millennium, marriages have varied structures, and although it continues to exist, a traditional marriage is undesirable or unattainable for many. Currently, there are three common types of family structures: intact *nuclear family*, single-parent family, and step/blended family.

Intact nuclear families, also known as the traditional family structure, consist of a mother, a father, and their biological children or their adopted children. Additionally, an intact nuclear family is one that is absent of divorce and in which membership has remained constant.

Single-parent families are those households that are led by one parent raising children alone. A single-parent household may consist of a single mother with her child(ren) or a single father with his child(ren). Sometimes, single-parent families can include other family members, such as grandparents, aunts, or uncles. However, the hallmark is the fact that the parent is raising the child(ren) without a partner. Although single-parent households are common across all races in the United States, the rate is highest among Black people. The Center for Immigration Studies reported that, in 2015, nearly 77 percent of Black births were to unwed mothers.

Step/blended families are created when individuals who have children from a previous marriage or relationship choose to marry. Commonly defined, a stepfamily is one in which only one member of the couple has a prior child(ren) before marriage. A blended family entails two separate families joining to form one new unit. In a blended stepfamily, both members of the couple had pre-existing children or the couple may have additional children together. According to the website Smart Stepfamilies, nearly 40 percent of Americans are part of a stepfamily. For African Americans, the high rate of unwed births creates an increased potential for a more "complex" blended stepfamily structure.

Cohabitation, commonly known as living together, is also a frequent occurrence for African Americans and creates a subtype of blended families; although cohabitation might not be legally binding or recognized, it creates family dynamics identical to those in stepfamilies. This includes the likelihood of experiencing similar challenges and expectations that occur after marriage.

Given the aforementioned statistic regarding births to single mothers, there is an increased likelihood that African Americans who are dating or engaged will bring at least one child into the relationship or were raised in a step/blended family themselves. There are many advantages to and strengths within stepfamilies. Likewise, there are many challenges that can surface when bringing two distinct family systems together. The change that happens after marriage is often difficult in itself. Joining families requires rapid changes in multiple areas of everyday life, and the newlywed couple has limited time together to adjust to the newness of their marital relationship. The strain on the adults and the children making the adjustment to their new life simultaneously can be extremely disorienting and stressful.

Each family has its own shared past and pre-existing way of being together, and they bring those into the new union wholly. When a stepfamily is formed, the members have no shared family histories and begin to build those histories with each interaction. Additionally, they often have very different beliefs regarding discipline, behavioral expectations, routine, religion, and, quite frankly, family.

Regardless of the age of the children, they may feel torn between their biological parents in a myriad of ways. For example, a child may feel torn between the parent they live with most/more of the time and the other parent who they visit. They may withhold affection from the new stepparent for fear of "hurting" the parent who is not in the household. Sadly, this is a very common occurrence in step/blended families and can cause major conflict in the couple's relationship.

It is important that you take the opportunity to discuss and plan for the joining of your families. This process requires that you reflect on and express your own experiences with, beliefs about, desires for, and fantasies of stepfamilies.

THE PAST

Experiences with and messages received about step/blended families when you were growing up can have an impact on how you approach them now and in the future. For example, if you were raised by a loving stepparent, you might think that blending a family is easy. Conversely, if you were raised in a two-parent household with loving parents, you might believe that children can only be raised and loved by their biological parents. Although your thoughts and beliefs might not be as concrete as these examples, your past will definitely affect how you approach your future family; therefore, it is important to think about the past. Begin by defining your family of origin.

I describe my family while I was growing up as (check one):
- ☐ Nuclear family (Mom and Dad were married to each other, and all my siblings and I have the same parents).
- ☐ Single-parent household (One parent in the household was primarily responsible for my care).
- ☐ Extended-family single-parent household (One parent was primarily responsible for my care, and other extended family—grandparents, aunts, uncles, cousins—lived in the household).
- ☐ Stepfamily (My biological parent(s) married someone who didn't have children of their own).
- ☐ Blended family (My biological parent(s) married someone with children or they had children together).

What messages did you receive about step/blended families while you were growing up? (This could be from the media, family, friends.) What did you experience, see, or hear about stepparents and stepchildren? _____

_____

_____

_____

_____

Which of those messages still come up when you think about becoming a stepfamily? _____

_____

_____

_____

_____

THE PRESENT

Current circumstances are as important as your past. How your life is structured now will affect the level of change you will experience after marriage. Shifting from being a single parent to parenting with a "new" partner or moving from being single and childless to instant parenthood of an already-formed human can be a jarring transition. When you are dating and not living together, it can be pretty easy to separate your relationship with the children from your relationship with your partner. For instance, you can schedule *all* your dates and alone time when the children are being cared for by others. You and your partner might not have had to stop your interactions to comfort an upset child or to intervene in sibling conflict. Similarly, you might not have been put in a position to say no to your partner's child or to hear your partner say no to your child. This current phase can be quite pleasant—so pleasant that you might be reluctant to think about the inevitable shift that will occur when you begin to co-parent.

Additionally, current relationships with those involved in the life of the child can be a signal for what's to come. Entering into a serious relationship can stir up negative feelings in ex-spouses/ex-partners that can cause major conflicts. These conflicts have the potential to not only affect the relationship between the ex-partners but also disrupt your current relationship and interfere with budding relationships with the children. Taking stock of how the children's "other" parent is responding to the introduction of new people into the child's life and exploring how your current lifestyle might support or hinder the joining of your families are important steps to planning the future. The following exercises will help you begin to think about how you are currently blending your families.

Begin by describing your current circumstances.

⊙ Currently, I have _____ children by _____ ex-partners.
        (number of children)   *(number of partners)*

♥ My child(ren) (check one):
   ☐ Live with me 100 percent of the time.
   ☐ I have joint custody with their other biological parent.
   ☐ Live with me part-time because I have joint custody with their other biological parent.
   ☐ Visit their other biological parent (check one):
      ☐ Consistently
      ☐ Occasionally
      ☐ Rarely
      ☐ Never

⊙ If you currently have relationships and responsibilities for children who are not biologically your own, describe the relationship and your commitment (time, money, energy): _____

_____

_____

_____

_____

_____

_____

_____

♥ Currently, my ex-partner has _____ children by _____ partners.
        (number of children)   *(number of partners)*

♥ My ex-partner's child(ren) (check one):
   ☐ Live with me 100 percent of the time.
   ☐ Live part-time with me because I have joint custody.
   ☐ Have a set visitation schedule with their other biological parent.
   ☐ Visit their other biological parent (check one):
      ☐ Consistently
      ☐ Occasionally
      ☐ Rarely
      ☐ Never

How have custody/visitation schedules or a lack thereof had an impact on your relationship with each other and the children? _____

_____
_____
_____
_____
_____
_____
_____
_____

What can be done now to ensure that you and your partner have time alone to build your relationship and marriage? _____

_____
_____
_____
_____
_____
_____
_____

I pay/receive $_____ per month in child support. It is important to discuss how child support will be handled in relation to the household assets/accounts.

I owe back child support in the total amount of $_____. It is important to discuss how back child support will be paid and whether it has or will negatively affect your lifestyles (e.g., credit report, driver's license, passport).

If your child(ren) has met your current partner, how would you describe their relationship? (Think about the level of expressed warmth, conflict, acceptance, rejection, etc.) _____

_____
_____
_____
_____
_____
_____
_____

If you have met your partner's child(ren), how would you describe the relationship? (Think about the level of expressed warmth, conflict, acceptance, rejection, etc.). _____

_____

_____

_____

_____

_____

_____

Describe your relationship with your ex-partner/co-parent:
How do you communicate (text, phone, in person)? _____
How often do you communicate? _____
How would you describe the quality and dynamics of your relationship (e.g., pleasant, conflicted, toxic)? Explain. _____

_____

_____

_____

_____

_____

_____

_____

_____

_____

How does your ex-partner feel about your being in a relationship with your partner, and how is it expressed? _____

_____

_____

_____

_____

_____

_____

_____

_____

THE FUTURE

Your past experiences and your current lifestyle both influence your fantasies and expectations of your future family. When imagining the future, you might envision that everyone will instantaneously love each other, that you and your partner will agree on how to raise the children, or that you'll never question your choice to marry. The reality is that sometimes children do not like their stepparent and vice versa and that you will have differences of opinion about raising children, and you might find yourself asking, "Why did I get married?" even if for a fleeting moment.

Just as adults fantasize about having a "whole" family, many children have fantasies of their own. Unfortunately, most adults assume that children's fantasies are similar to theirs. However, each member of a newly formed family brings a complex set of expectations, fantasies, and desires with them. The adult's fantasy might be "I love my partner, and my children will love them just the same, and we will be one big happy family." And, regardless of their ages, the children may have fantasies that are the complete opposite of the adults'. The children might fantasize about their parents getting back together, and therefore see the stepparent as a threat. They may believe in the trope of the evil stepmother. They might dream about going back to a time when it was just their single parent and them. The family may even begin to organize along biological lines, creating "us" against "them" alliances. It is important for us to mention that these challenges can and do occur with adult children as well. Adult children may even have a more vested interest in their parents' remarriage and have more "power" to say so. They may feel fears of abandonment, loss, and change just like little ones do. Having direct conversations and including them in your new relationship can help in the transition to becoming a "family."

This felt sense of how it should be often inhibits the ability to relinquish these fantasies and accept the realities of the imperfect family. Abandoning the fantasy of a "perfectly" blended family represents the loss of a dream and might trigger feelings associated with the loss of a previous marriage or committed relationship. In many ways, the fantasy represents the potential for hope and healing. However, fantasy devoid of both challenges and triumphs can lead to major disappointment and feelings of hopelessness. Hopelessness can lead to reduced effort, withdrawal, and increased conflict, all of which can have an impact on the success of the marriage. To combat this, you must verbalize the unspoken and make room for a reality that might look very different from the fantasy but that can be just as gratifying.

The exercises in this section are a little different. You and your partner should review and discuss the questions not only with each other but also with the children who will be coming into the marriage. It is important to give them a space to discuss their fantasies and fears about the new family. Additionally, you all can share your own fantasies about your new family and begin to discuss a plan for how you'll handle challenges that will inevitably occur.

Describe the fantasies you have about the joining of your two families. _____

_____
_____
_____
_____
_____
_____
_____
_____
_____
_____
_____
_____
_____
_____
_____
_____
_____
_____
_____

Describe the fears or concerns you have about the joining of your two families that you have not shared yet. _____

_____
_____
_____
_____
_____
_____
_____
_____
_____
_____
_____
_____
_____
_____
_____
_____
_____
_____

List some expectations you have of each person (partner, children, stepchildren, co-parent). _____

_____

_____

_____

_____

_____

_____

_____

_____

What are some expectations you think your partner has of you as a parent or stepparent? _____

_____

_____

_____

_____

_____

_____

_____

_____

_____

What are some expectations you think your children have of you? _____

_____

_____

_____

_____

_____

_____

_____

_____

What are some expectations you think your stepchildren have of you? _____

_____

_____

_____

_____

_____

_____

_____

_____

After completing this chapter, you and your partner should continue to have open and ongoing conversations about the challenges and triumphs associated with blending. Areas for continued discussion include:

- How will children refer to the stepparent? What will they be called?
- How will discipline be handled?
- How will you make space for the children's thoughts and feelings?
- How will interactions with the other biological parent be managed?

Many experts say that, under the best circumstances, it takes about five to seven years for a family to blend. So be patient. Blending a family can have its challenges. However, it can also bring many rewards. With forethought, flexibility, and patience—sprinkled with large doses of reality—you all can function as a healthy family unit. By managing expectations and taking time to see things from the other's perspective, you can create an environment for love and connection to grow. It is important not to force yourself or others to fit into a fantasy-inspired picture, like the Brady bunch. Work with what you have, given the context of your reality, to develop a picture of family for yourselves.

As a result of your weekly discussion:

Our identified strengths in this area are: _____

_____

_____

_____

_____

The things that we need to continue to talk about in this area are: _____

_____

_____

_____

_____

What are your next steps? How will you work on your growth areas? Write down your plan of action. For example, will you seek help from others (i.e., a counselor, therapist, or mentor), or will you two read, study, and discuss together as a couple? _____

_____

_____

_____

_____

_____

_____

Resources for further information on blended families:

- *Building Love Together in Blended Families: The 5 Love Languages and Becoming Stepfamily Smart* by Gary Chapman and Ron L. Deal (2020).
- *Step Parenting: 50 One-Minute DOs and DON'Ts for Stepdads and Stepmoms* by Randall Hicks (2016).
- *The Blended Family Activity Book: 75 Fun Activities to Help Families Connect and Spend Time Together* by Julie Johnson (2022).

CHAPTER 7

Blood and Water (Extended Family)

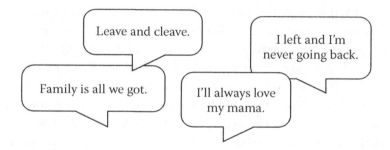

ig Mama's house for Sunday dinners: all the cousins sleeping on floor pallets because no one wanted to go home, always someone at the family gathering whom you have no idea how you're related to—sound familiar? Many African Americans, especially those closer to their southern roots, were raised in multigenerational households or in close proximity (on the same block or in the same apartment complex) to their extended family. Additionally, most can still name a nonbiologically related "relative" who holds a family title: Aunt Sharon who is mom's best friend or Cousin Big D, the son of the neighbor who grew up next door. Often these nonbiologically related relatives, known as *fictive kin/*

kinfolk, are just as connected to the "family" as blood relatives and have familial input, rights, and responsibilities.

Although some researchers have documented the existence of fictive kin family structures in some West African villages prior to American enslavement, the practice became vital to physical, psychological, and emotional survival for enslaved Africans. During American enslavement, families were purposefully separated for various reasons, including financial gain, punishment, or to prevent cohesion, which could lead to rebellion. Hence, enslaved Africans filled the void left by their absent extended family with kinfolk, to re-create the supportive family structures and hierarchy found in biological families. These families of choice were beneficial for all involved. Older people were able to continue their contributions to the community by assuming the role of grandparent, women and men gained brothers and sisters, children gained a host of adults who assisted in their care, and, most importantly, people found a sense of belonging and connectedness.

This practice has survived in the African American community over the years. However, currently, due in part to *assimilation* or the taking on of a more westernized, individually focused mindset, this tradition is not as widely observed by the younger generation. Migration from small southern towns to large urban cities for better opportunities has led to greater exposure to and reward for Western European values, which emphasize self-sufficiency of the nuclear family.

Those who hold more-traditional beliefs about extended family and kinfolk might view these relationships as a necessary part of life. They may continue to create family throughout their lifetime and thrive as part of a large network for whom they have responsibility and garner support. Alternatively, those who hold more-modern beliefs about the primacy of the nuclear family (Mom, Dad, and children) might devalue the importance of extended family and fail to recognize kinfolk as such.

Differing attitudes about family makeup, relations, and involvement can be a major source of a couple's conflict. Extended family and kinfolk can either be a support to the marriage, an impartial entity, or a source of stress to the marriage/relationship. In addition to providing love, connection, and support, they can come with rules and expectations that tax resources and serve as a persistent strain on marriages. The expectations of extended family might include sharing financial resources with struggling family members, caring for others' children when they are unable, engaging in family drama, and holding family secrets. Conversely, relying only on the nuclear family can be overwhelming, isolating, and limiting. The limited resources of the couple can become taxed without trusted others to provide relief. Without an extended family network, the couple has sole responsibility for all aspects of their life, with minimal access to assistance when distressed.

Exploring each other's expectations regarding the involvement of and connection to extended family and kinfolk can prevent partners from feeling like they have to choose between their family and their relationship.

THE PAST

American enslavement had a huge impact on the daily life of African Americans. Most had no choice but to have close connections to others in order to survive. Depending on when and where you were born, you may have had more personal experience with this level of interconnectedness. Historically, African Americans were excluded from the government resources and protections afforded to other US citizens; therefore, the extended family and kinfolk did what the government would not. Things like informal adoption, leaving children with relatives as parents migrated north and west looking for better opportunities, and having Grandma in a hospital bed in the living room rather than in a nursing home were commonplace. Some embraced and carried on that tradition, and others have chosen not to. It is also important to acknowledge that not everyone has pleasant memories of loving, supportive, helpful families. For some, family was the source of their greatest trauma and tragedy. Given that most abuse experienced in childhood, including physical, sexual, and emotional abuse, is inflicted by someone the child knows, the perpetrators are usually family members. Therefore, the word "family" does not conjure up the same feelings and memories for everyone.

You must spend time thinking about how family was "done" when you were growing up. What messages were you given about extended family and family friends? What comes up for you when you think about family? All these questions are important because they help to uncover what has shaped your vision for your future family.

I'd describe my relationship with my extended family (grandparents, aunts/ uncles, cousins) while growing up as (check one):

- ☐ Extremely close (saw or talked to each other almost daily, lived close together, stayed at each other's homes frequently; I knew almost everybody).
- ☐ Somewhat close (gathered for holidays, kept in contact by phone often, knew what was happening with each other, called if we needed something; I knew the majority of my family).
- ☐ Somewhat distant (saw family every few years, only gathered for weddings and funerals; I knew most people by sight but not by name).
- ☐ Extremely distant (didn't see extended family for years while growing up; I wouldn't know most of them if I saw them).

Describe your experiences with family while you were growing up. _____

_____

_____

_____

_____

_____

_____

_____

_____

_____

_____

_____

_____

_____

_____

_____

_____

_____

_____

_____

_____

_____

_____

_____

How did you feel about the time you spent with extended family while grow-ing up? Are your memories mostly pleasant and joyous, sad and lonely, or a mixture of both? _____

_____

_____

_____

_____

Did you ever wish for the time you spent with family to be different? More family around? Less family around? Less drama? _____

_____

_____

_____

THE PRESENT

As you have moved into adulthood, you have had the opportunity to make your own decisions about how you relate to others. Some of us make a conscious decision to form the types of connections that we have. Others of us simply act and behave in a way that is familiar to us, which influences how our relationships take shape. Think about your current relationships with your family members. Simply put, the transition to adulthood, ideally, gives you more choices. You can decide how financially, physically (e.g., Do you move out?), and emotionally dependent you are on those who raised you. You also get to decide how involved they are in your life and how much responsibility you take on for their care as they get older. Many don't make this choice consciously; they continue to do what has always been done and may end up relating to their family members in the same way they did when they were ten years old.

For example, some may talk to their parents multiple times a day, just like they did when they were growing up. Others have completely distanced themselves from their family because they still carry resentment for things that happened during their childhood. Neither having constant communication with your family nor being estranged from them is inherently problematic. But both have the potential to affect your intimate relationship with your partner, especially if your partner has a very different idea of how "to do" family. Taking time to think about your current relationships with your family members can help uncover your beliefs and desires about integrating extended family into your future life with your partner.

Think about your current relationships with your family members and kinfolk and answer the questions below.

 I'd describe my current relationships with my extended family (grandparents, aunts/uncles, cousins) as (check one):

- ☐ Extremely close (see or talk to each other almost daily, live close together, stay at each other's homes frequently; I know almost everybody).
- ☐ Somewhat close (gather for holidays, keep in contact by phone often, know what is happening with each other, call if we need something; I know the majority of my family).
- ☐ Somewhat distant (see family every few years, only gather for weddings and funerals; I know most people by sight but not by name).
- ☐ Extremely distant (don't see extended family for years; I wouldn't know most of them if I saw them).

Read through the items in the following list. Check all that apply and compare your answers.

- ☐ I currently spend holidays and special occasions with extended family.
- ☐ I visit with members of my family at least weekly.
- ☐ Family must call before they come by.
- ☐ I send my children to spend an extended period of time with family during the summers/holidays.
- ☐ I currently live with members of my family (other than my children).
- ☐ I give or receive money from my family when needed.
- ☐ I currently live in the same state as many of my extended family members.
- ☐ When my family comes to town, they stay with me.
- ☐ I talk to someone in my family by phone or text at least weekly.
- ☐ Extended family members are allowed to discipline my kids.

How are your current interactions with family similar and dissimilar to what you experienced while growing up? Do you ever wish for it to be different?

_____
_____
_____
_____
_____

Has the way you "do" family interfered with your relationship with your current or past partner(s)? If so, how? _____
_____
_____
_____
_____
_____

Do you see this continuing to be an issue? (It is important for you and your partner to communicate and develop strategies for managing/changing this dynamic.) _____
_____
_____
_____
_____
_____

THE FUTURE

As you are planning your future family, now is the time to begin to make conscious decisions about the roles and level of involvement of your extended family and kinfolk. You and your partner should share your desires, as well as boundaries, for your loved ones. It is also important to have conversations with your family to relay your decisions to them. As you move toward marriage, it is important for you, your partner, and those closest to you to expect and plan for changes in the relationship. Remember that your needs and desires may change over time, so keep the lines of communication open.

Think of boundaries as personal guidelines for how you expect to be treated by others, including your family. As you build a family of your own, you must think about how your family should be treated. We often hear the African proverb, "It takes a village to raise a child," so many may be reluctant to set boundaries with their family because they are afraid to upset them or lose their support. We must remember that even villages have rules that govern how members relate to each other. The joining of two families makes discussing boundaries with family that much more important.

As you think about your future relationships with extended family members, consider additional discussions around financial responsibility for family members; living proximity; care for aging/ill parents, siblings, or others; holiday gatherings; comfort with home visits, and so on.

After I am married, I would like my relationship with my extended family (grandparents, aunts/uncles, cousins) to be (check one):

☐ Extremely close (see or talk to each other almost daily, live close together, stay at each other's homes frequently; I know almost everybody).

☐ Somewhat close (gather for holidays, keep in contact by phone often, know what is happening with each other, call if we need something; I know the majority of my family).

☐ Somewhat distant (see family every few years, only gather for weddings and funerals; I know most people by sight but not by name).

☐ Extremely distant (don't have to see extended family for years; I don't need to know most of them at all).

Read through the items in the following list. Check all that apply and compare your answers.

☐ I want to spend holidays and special occasions with extended family.

☐ I am open to moving out of state for work.

☐ Family must call before they come by.
☐ I would like to send my children to spend an extended period of time with family during the summers/holidays.
☐ If my parents or other older kinfolk become ill, they can move in with us.
☐ Family can have a key to our home.
☐ I do not need to live in the same state with my family to be happy.
☐ I am okay with helping out if a family member needs a place to stay.

As you complete this chapter, remember that families are unique. Your family is not and cannot be used as the blueprint for how a family "should be." Make space for the wide variety of family dynamics that exist and be open to creating a new way of shaping family interactions and closeness with your partner. Remember that extended family can be both a source of support and a source of stress. Be honest with yourself, your partner, and your family about how you envision your future with them.

———————————

As a result of your weekly discussion:

Our identified strengths in this area are: _____
_____
_____
_____
_____
_____

The things that we need to continue to talk about in this area are:
_____
_____
_____
_____
_____

What are your next steps? How will you work on your growth areas? Write down your plan of action. For example, will you seek help from others (i.e., a counselor, therapist, or mentor), or will you two read, study, and discuss together as a couple? _____
_____
_____
_____

Resources for further information on extended families:

- _Boundaries: When to Say Yes, How to Say No to Take Control of Your Life_ (Updated and Expanded Edition) by Henry Cloud and John Townsend (2017).
- _The Black Extended Family_ by Elmer P. Martin and Joanne Mitchell Martin (1978).

CHAPTER 8

In To Me You See (Intimacy and Sex)

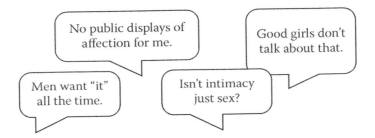

No public displays of affection for me.

Good girls don't talk about that.

Men want "it" all the time.

Isn't intimacy just sex?

Sex is one of the first things that comes to mind when we think of intimacy. However, intimacy and sex are not the same. A couple can have sex without true intimacy, and a couple can have intimacy without sex. These differences are important because most couples state that intimacy is needed in order for sex to be fulfilling. Sadly, sex is also historically one of the most taboo topics to talk about, especially in the Black community. Perhaps you heard messages while growing up like "You fass'," or "Don't bring home no babies." Additionally, there are other experiences that taught us about sex and how to feel about sex. For example, if you grew up in the church, it is likely that you heard messages about waiting until marriage and that sex or pregnancy out of wedlock was sinful and a disgrace. In other instances, you may have been socialized with different expectations based on your gender. For males, sex and "sex talk" have been more normalized, and "locker room talk" has become expected; for females, it is shameful and "unladylike." For many of us, sex was something briefly covered in health class during school and was focused on pregnancy and sexually transmitted diseases and infections, but it was never talked about as a healthy, human need.

Beyond messages about sex, many of us were not openly taught about what intimacy truly means. We may have observed intimacy in relationships around us without realizing it. Maybe it was that couple who finished each other's sentences, or maybe it was one of your parents who always seemed to be aware of how the other was feeling simply by the look in their eyes. Or perhaps it was the way they held hands as they sat and watched TV. Before we continue, we should define and highlight various types of intimacy.

The word "intimacy" is derived from the Latin *intimus*, which means "inner" or "inmost." As such, intimacy refers to sharing with others that which is inmost. This sharing fosters feelings of attachment, closeness, connectedness, and bondedness. Below are some of the ways that people can experience intimacy with another.

- *Emotional intimacy* is the sharing of innermost feelings with your partner. This includes open, honest, and transparent communication about feelings and desire, joys and pain.
- *Spiritual intimacy* encompasses sharing and connecting with your partner around spiritual beliefs.
- *Sexual intimacy* is a close sensual relationship. It ensures that both partners derive pleasure from the sexual act, allowing your bodies to express and experience the love and passion you feel for each other.
- *Physical intimacy* is different than the sexual act. It encompasses displays of affection toward each other through physical touch and contact other than the act of sex, such as holding hands, cuddling, kissing, hugging, or caressing an arm or waistline as you walk by one another.

If you have already completed the previous chapters, you will recall reading about the deep impact that enslavement left on Black families. In addition to gender roles, financial status, and belief systems, enslavement left a significant impact on our bodies and our ability to feel safe and to have a voice and power over our bodies. Experiences of physical and sexual violence created a legacy of trauma that had an impact on how Black couples engaged in intimacy and sex, and passed down both strength in how to stay safe and messages of trauma that taught us to be overly guarded at times. These experiences affected our ability to have positive feelings about our bodies and our understanding of sex as a normal, healthy, and safe activity. Furthermore, you may also recall that these experiences contributed to internalized racism and stereotypes about our bodies. Messages such as Black women are overly sexual/promiscuous or Black men have above-average-sized genitalia are examples of stereotypical messages that continue to endure. Some have learned to combat these messages by downplaying our sexuality and sexual desires altogether, by pretending to be needless and wantless. In some ways, having open discussions about sex reinforces the stereotypes about our sexual morality and causes feelings of guilt and shame. Generations have been taught not to talk about sex, not even to their spouses. Although sex is not being talked about, it is being engaged in. Unfortunately, a lack of open communication about sex can lead to poor marital satisfaction and an increase in marital conflicts.

Historical experiences also had an impact on open displays of vulnerability, which are building blocks for intimacy. In many instances, emotional openness and the expression of warm feelings often created an open door for the white enslavers to take advantage and invoke more violence. For example, threats to sell away a loved one could be used to keep an enslaved person in-line and obedient. "I see the way you look at him. If you don't do what I say, he gon' be gone tomorrow." In response, a person would hide feelings and affections for fear of being targeted. Outward shows of love and affection became dangerous, and over generations, this fear was passed down through parenting and how we interacted with loved ones; it became the norm.

This affected the awareness/emotional availability that we have and our willingness to be vulnerable with our partner. It is important for us to ask ourselves if we are open and willing to share emotions and things about us and our pasts, or if we hide things about ourselves from our partners. How we share our feelings and affection toward our partner can also be an issue. Sometimes we forget that the walls we keep to protect ourselves also serve to keep others out, including our partners. And this directly affects our ability for closeness and intimacy, which ultimately has an impact on our sex lives with and our emotional connections to our partners.

We all want a relationship that results in safety, peace, and trust but are often unaware of the blind spots that interfere with that deeper level of intimacy. In order for emotional vulnerability and sex to feel like a safe space in your relationship, a deeper understanding about intimacy must be established. This happens by exploring how you show up as an emotional, spiritual, and physical being in your relationship. This also happens by becoming more aware of any negative messages and experiences you have had in your sexual and emotional past. This will help you get to the goal of normalizing conversations about your intimate needs, while decoupling feelings of fear and shame.

In addition to historical racial trauma, according to research, many women and men have experienced sexual violence in their lifetimes. This can have a major impact on vulnerability and the various forms of intimacy. Before beginning your exploration of the past, present, and future, you must make room for the acknowledgment of any past trauma that you or your partner may have experienced. Without acknowledgment, past trauma creates room for unintentional disconnections and shutting your partner out without understanding the reason.

⚭ Respond to the statements below by placing a check mark in the appropriate box.

	Yes	No	Not Applicable
I've experienced emotional/verbal trauma in my past.			
I've experienced sexual trauma in my past.			
I have disclosed my past trauma to my partner.			
If I have not disclosed my past trauma to my partner, but I am ready to do so now.			
I believe my trauma may have an impact on our intimacy experiences.			

If you have not disclosed your past trauma to your partner and are not yet ready to do so, have a discussion with your partner and agree to what may constitute healthy and safe boundaries for you two. If your partner is not ready to disclose their trauma, your ability to respect their boundaries and process will contribute to the ongoing establishment of safety in the relationship.

🦋 If your partner is not ready to disclose, do you agree to respect their boundaries?   ☐Yes ☐No

THE PAST

Our upbringing and historical context have a profound impact on our ability to understand and create intimacy in our dating and marital relationships. Our previous observation of how our parents or other couples in our childhood engaged with one another served as our first examples of intimacy in a romantic relationship. They were our first examples of how to communicate emotions, show physical affection, and model vulnerability. We observed these behaviors many times through their actions. We were likely able to tell when our caregivers were getting along well and really vibing, as well as when they may not have been getting along; how we observed them cope or communicate, whether on good or bad days, affected our ability to be vulnerable and express our emotions. Without intentional communication and comfort within ourselves to navigate our truths, we may have difficulty exploring true intimacy with our partners. This can affect how we experience pleasure, the ability to give our partner feedback when we don't feel comfortable, and the creation of a trusting foundation in our relationships. Furthermore, if there were any instances of pain or abuse experienced from those who were supposed to love you, it will be important to separate those experiences from your definition of love and intimacy. Having blind spots in our intimate relationships can unintentionally trigger feelings of insecurity and a lack of safety and can contribute to becoming distanced over time. These first exercises will create opportunities for you to explore your early observations and understanding of intimacy.

Think about some examples of intimate relationships during your upbringing. What types of intimacy did you observe (emotional, spiritual, physical)? Describe. _____

_____
_____
_____
_____
_____
_____
_____

Now think about your own experiences of learning about physical and sexual intimacy. Who or what resources taught you about sexual intimacy and sexual activity? _____

_____
_____
_____
_____
_____
_____
_____
_____

What were some of the early messages you heard about sex? Were they positive and uplifting? Or were they shaming and negative? Explain. _____

_____
_____
_____
_____
_____
_____
_____
_____

How has your religious upbringing affected your views and beliefs about intimacy and sex? _____

_____

_____

_____

_____

_____

_____

_____

_____

_____

What were your first memories of seeing intimacy or sex portrayed in the media (e.g., music, movies, porn)? Were men represented differently than women? Were Black people portrayed differently than white people? _____

_____

_____

_____

_____

_____

_____

_____

_____

_____

_____

In thinking about your past, it is imperative to consider any instances of past trauma as well. Going through these exercises may bring up the challenging topic of sexual abuse, yet it is important to acknowledge and work through that as you are thinking about your future with your partner. Past abuse can have an impact on our ability to be present, to trust our partners, or to feel as though we can experience the pleasurable aspects of sex and intimacy. If this applies to you, disclosing this to a professional and then to your partner will be a very important aspect in healing and being available to build true intimacy. This will also help you and your partner understand how to prevent unintentional harm and triggers. When we are triggered, we project emotions or behaviors on our partners because it reminds us of past pain or an abuser. Disclosure will be a big part of your healing and establishment of safety. Although historically a taboo topic, sexual trauma happens and does not make you any less lovable, desirable, or worthy of a loving, healthy relationship.

THE PRESENT

In your current relationship, you have likely experienced some level of intimacy that has piqued your interest in taking this journey with your partner. Perhaps you feel a deep emotional connection, and you feel you can tell your partner "anything." Perhaps you have a strong physical attraction, and you have been engaging in aspects of physical touch or sexual activity. Whatever you are feeling about your partner deserves the space for authentic and clear understanding. There may be areas within yourself and your relationship that are unintentional blind spots to an even deeper connection than what you have. This is also important when gender is taken into consideration. Men and women are socialized differently, with different expectations of vulnerability and intimacy. Women are often categorized as more emotional and given a lot of room to show emotion and to be vulnerable. On the other hand, men are expected to be "strong" and to not cry, and have often heard negative stereotypes about showing any type of emotion other than anger. However, many Black women have been taught to be "strong" and "independent" and that vulnerability is a sign of weakness, which can also cause challenges. But this same emotional armor is what shielded us from a society that sought to take us out. Now we have to learn to lower our shields with each other. Our emotions are actually what we have in common across gender, and creating a safe space for both parties to experience and communicate them is essential.

Before someone else can truly see you, it is important to first see yourself. The more comfortable you are with your own vulnerability, the more comfortable you will be with your partner and their emotions.

 Using the types of intimacy defined above, fill in the boxes with examples of how you express each type of intimacy and how you would like your partner to express each with you.

Types of Intimacy	How Do You Express?	How Does Your Partner Express?	Notes
Emotional			

Types of Intimacy	How Do You Express?	How Does Your Partner Express?	Notes
Spiritual			
Sexual			
Physical			

All levels of intimacy require a sense of safety, while maintaining the expectation that everything will not always be perfect. Safety is the common thread that will allow us to show up fully "naked" in our relationship. Without that safety, barriers are built over time, and we remain guarded from one another.

⚭ This next exercise explores a few examples of intimacy and how you would rate your current experience with your partner. On a scale of 1–10, rate each item according to your feelings and experiences with your partner. One means you strongly disagree or struggle with this item, whereas 10 means it is a strength and happens with ease. After you have rated each item, use the "Comments" column to write down anything that comes up for you.

Intimacy in My Relationship	Scale of 1–10	Comments
I can talk to my partner about my emotions.		
I am comfortable with my partner talking about their emotions.		
I can talk to my partner about my body parts and appearance.		
I can talk to my partner about my sexual desires.		
The amount of physical touch we share is just right.		
I am comfortable giving feedback to my partner about sex, pleasure, and preferences.		
I am comfortable being naked around my partner.		
My partner makes me feel like I can tell him/her anything.		
I am comfortable disagreeing with my partner.		
I am able to receive feedback from my partner about my presence in our relationship.		

We all have some blind spots and areas of growth that our relationship will certainly reveal to us, whether now or in the future. We will now explore what potentially blocks your ability to be vulnerable and to let your true self show up.

 Check any of the items on this list that may apply to you and then make a commitment to yourself and your relationship to heal those areas. If you have things to add that are not on the list, be sure to identify those too. Challenge yourself to really think about intimacy and if any of these items have ever interfered with your ability to show up in your relationships.

Intimacy Blockers
Experiences in a past relationship.
History of abuse.
Rejection/abandonment by parent(s)/caregiver(s).
Body image issues (feeling like you are too big or too small, unattractive, etc.).
Self-esteem/self-worth (e.g., feeling like "I'm not good enough" or "I'm unlovable").
Racial trauma (experiences of racism or racial stereotypes).
Unresolved conflict with others or your partner.
Growing up in an unsafe or chaotic environment.
Unhealthy communication patterns.
Anger/resentment about the past.
Not feeling truly seen or desired.
Significant grief/loss.
History of being criticized or feeling unheard/undervalued.
Fear of getting close to others.

Hopefully, these exercises helped you to identify some areas of strength, areas of growth, and any barriers to your ability to fully connect with your partner. No matter your findings, each time you come together and discuss your activities, it is an investment in practicing intimacy.

THE FUTURE

As you go forward in your relationship, think about what continuing to build intimacy may look like for you two. The goal is to identify ways that you need help feeling safe and confident within the relationship. As discussed, that may require some work around removing shame, working through past trauma, or developing a more positive body image. This will also require you to be honest with your partner about where you are in your journey. Helping your partner to better understand you and gain insight into your inner workings can help them to feel safe and even more comfortable with you. Sentiments filled with empathy and compassion become more readily available when we have greater insight into our partners and their emotional needs.

⌒⌒ Use the next checklist to determine what your commitments will be for the wellness of your relationship.

Intimacy Builders
Laugh and have fun together.
Calendar time daily to connect.
Schedule regular, intentional, judgment-free check-ins with your partner.
Be open to feedback from your partner.
Practice communicating your needs.
Ask your partner what they need from you.
Find an individual and couples therapist.
Engage in physical touch without sex.
Kiss/hug every day before you leave the house.
Kiss/hug every day before you go to sleep.
Spend time connecting every week.

As you continue to explore what your commitment will be to strengthening and growing intimacy in your relationship, consider what you want the future and longevity of your relationship to embody. Many people use Gary Chapman's *The 5 Love Languages* to better understand how to love their partners and the many ways that love can be manifested and demonstrated to our partners. To truly see our partners, we must know and honor their inner workings and what speaks to their needs. This is an essential component for African American couples, as so much time is spent feeling unseen and invisible in the larger society. Our intimate relationships need to be a space where we feel the most safe, understood, and vulnerable.

⌒⌒ Take time to think about moments or gestures that make you feel truly loved in your relationship that you would like to see continued in the future. _____

_____

_____

_____

_____

_____

_____

_____

_____

_____

_____

_____

_____

_____

_____

_____

_____

_____

_____

_____

Now, think about your future sex life. It will be essential for you two to have ongoing communication about your sex lives, as with time our bodies, schedules, and needs change. To begin, use the table below to identify topics that will help you create ongoing communication about your sexual relationship as it evolves.

	Sex Life
	I feel fine scheduling sex with my partner.
	I am comfortable initiating sex.
	I want my partner to initiate sex.
	I will tell my partner as my body experiences changes.
	I want to explore different positions or other experimenting in our sex life.
	I want a spontaneous sex life.
	I only want to have sex in the bedroom, in the dark.
	I want to implement adult toys in our sex life.
	I will communicate things that turn me off in the bedroom.
	I want to flirt/talk about sex outside of sexual activity.
	I want to experience foreplay before sex.
	I want us to use birth control.

Consider these tips and tools for creating your own intimacy recipe; be honest and communicate your true needs and desires. The items below are examples to provide a starting place. Expecting your partner to read your mind or to "just know" is a setup for failure every time. In the examples, you will find suggestions or reminders to help you think about how to actively engage and continue building intimacy going forward.

Intimacy Tips and Tools

Emotional	• Engage in weekly check-ins. • Identify a safe word for when feeling overwhelmed. • Schedule time to share feelings. • Use "I" statements to communicate feelings and needs.
Mental	• Read a book together. • Talk about current events. • Learn a new skill or hobby together. • Work toward a common goal.
Spiritual	• Pray together. • Attend worship services or small groups together. • Share celebrations. • Sharing what you are grateful for/blessings with each other daily.
Physical	• Exercise together. • Discuss physical touch (preferences/boundaries). • Flirt with each other. • Offer compliments.
Sexual	• Ask questions and be curious about your partner's desires. • Be open to feedback. • Be spontaneous. • Communicate needs/desires. • Create your bedroom environment together.

Take these tools with you on your journey and remember to embrace the spirit of giving just as much as you expect to receive in your relationship. True intimacy starts within us as we explore ways to let our partners into our most inner, genuine self. The more comfortable you are with your own vulnerabilities, the more you create a safe, reassuring space for your partner.

You have completed another step to officially confirming your journey toward a healthy understanding of and foundation for intimacy in your relationship. The ideal goal is for you to have a clearer sense of the tools you need to build a stronger emotional, physical, spiritual, and sexual connection with your partner. Furthermore, we hope that you have a clearer vision of what future communication should include in the areas of intimacy. May you continue to build on these ingredients for a wonderful future of fulfilling, reciprocal intimacy.

As a result of your weekly discussion:

⊙⊙ Our identified strengths in this area are: _____

_____

_____

_____

_____

_____

⊙⊙ The things that we need to continue to talk about in this area are:

_____

_____

_____

_____

_____

⊙⊙ What are your next steps? How will you work on your growth areas? Write down your plan of action. For example, will you seek help from others (i.e., a counselor, therapist, or mentor), or will you two read, study, and discuss together as a couple? _____

_____

_____

_____

_____

_____

Resources for further information on intimacy:

- *Intimacy ≠ Sex: 180 Activities to Help Couples Connect* by Erica Holmes (2023).
- *The 5 Love Languages: The Secret to Love That Lasts* by Gary Chapman (2015).

FINAL WORDS

*C*ongratulations! By completing this workbook, you have taken concrete steps to invest in the future of your relationship. We hope that you use the insights and tools you've learned to help strengthen connection, communication, understanding, and commitment. We urge you to continue to explore your areas of growth and fortify your areas of strength. Take time to explore the suggested resources at the end of each chapter and research some of your own.

And why not keep it up? During this process, you have dedicated time weekly to spend with each other focusing on your relationship goals. It would be great for you to make that a habit. Continue to calendar time together each week to connect around the current and future state of your relationship.

Last, there is no shame in bringing in the professionals. If you find that you and your partner are having difficulty finding common ground in specific areas of your relationship, reach out to a mentor, faith leader, or therapist who specializes in working with couples. It is better to seek help before things get so severe that you are thinking about throwing in the towel.

We wish you well in your journey to happy, healthy, long-lasting love.

APPENDIX A

The Broom-Jumping Ceremony

INSTRUCTIONS

To be read at the end of the wedding ceremony by an officiant or an elder designated by the couple or family.

SAMPLE SCRIPT

Oral history tells us that the ancestral roots of the broom-jumping ritual began deep in the heart of Africa. It is said that broom jumping comes from a tribal marriage ritual of placing sticks on the ground to represent the couple's new home together and the joining of two families. Therefore, it is practiced with honor for the ancestors and the beauty of our rich heritage. Not only is the ritual itself symbolic but each of the various parts of the broom have symbolic meaning. The straws of the broom represent family; the handle represents the Almighty; and the ribbon represents the tie that binds the couple together.

Over the years, its original purpose, significance, and association with Africa have been lost, leaving many to believe that the tradition began during enslavement. However, broom jumping was one of the few traditions that the African enslaved were able to practice. And today in America, the broom-jumping ritual has been handed down from generation to generation to remind us of a time when our vows were not legally sanctioned. During enslavement, our ancestors sought the legitimacy of marriage by jumping over the broom and into the bonds of domesticity. For our ancestors, this small ritual was a legal and bonding act connecting them with the heritage of the homeland and giving legitimacy, dignity, and strength to their unions—sanctioning them by the Almighty.

Before the eyes of God and in the spirit of the ancestors, [insert groom's name] and [insert bride's name] publicly declare the joining of their families, the centrality of God, and that they are bound together as one.

Please join me as we count to three: one . . . two . . . three!

APPENDIX B

Using "I" Statements

Using "I" statements and avoiding criticism, defensiveness, contempt, and stonewalling in your communication will lay a foundation for developing healthy and productive interactions with your partner. These strategies will get you and your partner closer to creating the relationship you desire.

Think about a time when you and your partner did not communicate well. Let's practice using "I" statements. Complete the sentence below using your feelings at that time, the behavior you didn't like, and what you needed instead.

I feel _____ (insert feeling) when you _____ (insert specific statement or behavior); what I need from you is _____ (insert specific behavior or alternative response).

APPENDIX C

Glossary of Terms

Active listening—Listening and paying attention to what a speaker is communicating verbally, with the intent to understand the message. It includes observing body language and providing feedback that conveys understanding.

Allegory—A story, poem, or picture that can be interpreted to reveal a hidden meaning, typically a moral or political one.

Anti-Black racism—A specific kind of racial prejudice directed toward Black people; it acknowledges that not all ethnic groups have the same lived experience and focuses specifically on nuances of racism against the Black community.

Antidote—A remedy to counteract the effects of poison. It also relieves, prevents, or counteracts the effects of a negative event.

Assimilation—When people or groups of one culture come together and learn and absorb another culture's ideas, attitudes, and beliefs. For example, someone from another country comes to America and takes on American values and culture and erases all elements of their birth culture.

Atheist—A person who disbelieves or lacks belief in the existence of God.

Black church—The body of US Christian congregations and denominations that minister to the collective traditions of African Americans. It was created in response to a system designed to crush their spirit and subsequently became integral in fighting against that system.

Blended families—When two people come together in marriage with children from previous relationships/marriages to form an integrated family unit.

Clark Doll Study—A popular research study by Black psychologists (Kenneth and Mamie Clark, 1940s) that determined that positive and negative understandings of race begin in early childhood. The study found that all children, Black or white, are more likely to associate negative attributes toward a Black doll and positive attributes toward a white doll. Similar findings were established in a recent study.

Cultural oppression—The placing of untrue ideas, values, and beliefs about how to live or simply exist onto another culture. For example, this has caused members of the Black community to feel they have to act one way at work but are free to act "normal" at home.

Diaspora—A population of people from one geographical "home" who have been scattered around the globe. We often refer to the African diaspora and include all the places around the world where African descendants now reside. This includes North, Central, and South America and the Caribbean, to name a few.

Discrimination—Unfair or biased treatment of others based on race, gender, age, religion, or sexual orientation. The behavior can be obvious or subtle in day-to-day interactions.

Effective communication—The process of exchanging thoughts, feelings, and ideas and expressing emotions in a way that is mutually acknowledged and understood. The receiver clearly understands the message sent by the sender. Essentially, communication is a process of understanding and sharing meaning.

Egalitarian gender roles—Partners in the relationship share equal responsibility in the household, in parenting, and with finances. The couple works as a team, with flexibility.

Emotional awareness—The ability to recognize and make sense of your own emotions as well as the emotions of others.

Emotional temperature—Gauging or assessing your overall range of emotions and the intensity of emotions. On a scale of 1–10, 1 represents the lowest intensity, when you may feel relaxed and calm, while 10 represents the highest emotional intensity, when you may feel overwhelmed, frustrated, or angry. Communicating with a high emotional temperature can cause you to lose focus and may lead to serious misunderstandings with your partner.

Emotional vulnerability—The ability or willingness to acknowledge and express one's feelings. This includes both pleasant and unpleasant emotions and asking for what you need.

Enslavement—The act of white colonizers capturing African people and forcing them into slavery. We use the term "enslavement" to place emphasis on the actions of white colonizers as they enslaved Black people; "slave" is not an identity that Black people voluntarily take on.

Fictive kin—People who are not related by blood or marriage but who are considered family or extended family. There is a close emotional bond, and you have chosen to make them part of the family. An example would be a godparent or a "brother from another mother."

Financial transparency—The timely, meaningful, and reliable disclosure of your financial matters, habits, and status.

Four Horsemen of the Apocalypse—A metaphor used by John and Julie Schwartz Gottman to describe unhealthy communication styles that can be destructive to a relationship and often predict divorce or separation (criticism, defensiveness, contempt, stonewalling).

Gary Chapman—A popular couples expert and author who coined "The 5 Love Languages" (quality time, physical touch, receiving gifts, words of affirmation, acts of service) and wrote a book by the same name.

Gender roles—A range of socially acceptable and appropriate behaviors based on a person's assigned sex. For example, traditional gender roles state that girls/women are expected to take care of the home and be nurturing and soft and that men are expected to be strong and aggressive and to take care of the cars and bills.

Historical oppression—The chronic or repeated instances of oppression that may have become normalized and institutionalized over time. Examples include redlining, predatory lending, and challenges getting fair voting rights for Black people.

Intergenerational trauma—The trend of sending down patterns of traumatic or oppressive effects to younger generations. For example, sometimes Black parents discipline their children based on past styles of "respect" or out of fear, rather than on what might be healthy ways to respond to child behavior.

Internalized racism—A type of oppression; the tendency of Black people to believe stereotypes or beliefs about themselves based on the rules or norms defined by white people.

Intimacy—A state marked by emotional closeness.

Kinfolk—Family members with the same bloodline and ancestry. This includes distant family members whom you may have never met. We also expand this term to include fictive kin who are not biologically related but have all the rights and responsibilities as family members.

Marginalization—The treatment of a person or group as insignificant or on the outskirts.

Nigrescence—A racial identity model created by William E. Cross Jr. It identifies the process of becoming in touch with one's Blackness or identity as a Black person living in America.

Nuclear family—Parents and their biological or adopted children who live under one roof.

Oppression—The unjust or cruel exercise of authority or power to limit/block another group's access to advancement and resources.

Peony Fhagen-Smith—Developmental psychologist who was a contributor to the Model of Black Identity Development, with William E. Cross Jr.

Personal identity—Our understanding of our self-image and beliefs about ourselves, and how we differ from others.

Race salience—The level of importance race has to a person. For example, some people are strongly connected to being Black, whereas others are more connected to a general human experience or identity.

Racial discrimination—Prejudiced or unfair treatment of a person or a group based on their racial or cultural background.

Racial identity—The meaning, weight, and importance that being African American has in your life.

Racial oppression—Burdening a specific race with unjust or cruel restraints or impositions.

Sankofa—Meaning "go back and get it," Sankofa is a principle derived from the Akan people of Ghana that one should remember the past in order to make positive progress in the future. Represented either with a stylized heart shape or by a bird with its head turned backward while its feet face forward, carrying a precious egg in its mouth. Sankofa is often associated with the proverb, *Se wo were fi na wosankofa a yenkyi*, which translates as, "It is not wrong to go back for that which you have forgotten."

Self-soothing—Any behavior that a person can use to regulate their emotions and make themselves feel better. A few examples include taking deep breaths, listening to music, meditating, taking a walk, or squeezing a stress ball.

Stereotype—To unfairly believe that all people with specific traits or characteristics are the same.

Systemic and institutionalized racism—Racial discrimination practices that are built into almost every system in society, including criminal justice, housing, education, health care, employment, and politics.

Trauma—Experiencing an extremely frightening or distressing event that overwhelms a person's way of coping and may result in challenges in functioning or coping normally after the event. This includes instances of physical abuse/violence and psychological events such as racism. Each can lead to questioning of oneself and one's environment, difficulties trusting, challenges feeling safe, and struggles feeling calm or grounded.

Unhealthy communication—Communication that often involves blaming, defensiveness, and disrespectful language. Partners are talking "at" one another instead of "with" one another, and they are listening to their partner in order to "respond" instead of listening to "understand." It can be toxic, unproductive, and damaging to the relationship.

William E. Cross Jr.—Renowned researcher and psychologist in the study of identity development, specifically Black identity development and the nigrescence model.

ABOUT THE AUTHORS

 ERICA HOLMES, PSYD, is a licensed clinical psychologist who serves as the executive director of Champion Counseling Center at Faithful Central Bible Church, an associate program chair and the director of the Psychological Trauma Studies specialization in the master's in psychology program at Antioch University Los Angeles, and the founder of HOMMs Consulting. Her areas of inquiry and more than 150 presentations have focused on relationships and coupling, insight and empowerment, psychological trauma, psychotherapy with African American clients, and the integration of Christianity and psychology. She is an American Psychological Association Minority Fellow and past board member for the Los Angeles chapter of the Association of Black Psychologists. She is the author of *Dating with Purpose: A Single Woman's Guide to Escaping No Man's Land* and *Intimacy ≠ Sex: 180 Activities to Help Couples Connect* and a co-editor of the upcoming book *Black Couples Therapy: Clinical Theory and Practice* (Cambridge University Press). She can be reached at www.docerica.com.

 RONECIA LARK, PSYD, is a licensed clinical psychologist and a licensed marriage and family therapist. Dr. Lark has worked in various clinical settings, including in schools, community mental health, and children and family services. She has over fifteen years of experience teaching and training in academia as an adjunct professor in undergraduate and graduate programs in psychology, marriage and family therapy, and criminal justice. Dr. Lark has twenty-five years of prior law enforcement experience with an extensive background in working with diverse communities dealing with various life issues, such as crisis, trauma, domestic violence, victimology, and inclusion. Currently, Dr. Lark is the recruitment and training coordinator at the Champion Counseling Center in Inglewood, California, where she enjoys providing training and clinical supervision to master's and doctoral level students. While Dr. Lark enjoys working with individuals and families, her specific area of interest is in working with couples. She can be reached at www.drnecia.com.

 **JESSICA M. SMEDLEY, PSYD,** is a licensed clinical psychologist and owner of Smedley Psychological Services in Washington, DC. She holds adjunct faculty appointments at Howard University and The George Washington University. She also holds significant leadership roles in the American Psychological Association and the DC Psychological Association. Dr. Smedley's unique background includes an MA in counseling, with an emphasis on marriage and family therapy, and doctoral training completed at a seminary, with a focus on trauma and spirituality in urban communities. Dr. Smedley has given numerous presentations about racial trauma and wellness in Black communities, including the Black church, and has been seen on various media outlets offering insight about mental health and trauma. She is the author of *Dear Black Girl: Essential Guided Reflections to Celebrate You* and *Reclaiming Our Space: A Devotional Journal for the Black Woman of Faith.* She can be reached at www.smedleypsych.com.

Author portraits © 2022 Gregory Worsham Photography

Made in the USA
Middletown, DE
02 November 2023

41853618R00077